Toward the End

JOHN GERLACH

Toward the End

Closure and Structure
in the American Short Story

THE UNIVERSITY OF ALABAMA PRESS

Publication of this book was made possible,
in part, by financial assistance from
the Andrew W. Mellon Foundation and
the American Council of Learned Societies

Library of Congress Cataloging in Publication Data

Gerlach, John C.
  Towards the end.
  Bibliography: p.
  Includes index.
  1. Short stories, American—History and criticism.
  2. Fiction—Technique.   3. Plots (Drama, novel, etc.)
  I. Title.
  PS374.S5G37 1985   813'.01'09   84-2509
  ISBN 0-8173-0233-6
  ISBN 0-8173-0234-4 (pbk.)

For Lana, Brett, and Elizabeth,
and in memory of Elizabeth MacAndrew

Contents

Acknowledgments

I would like to thank several of my colleagues, in particular Barton Friedman, Cynthia Edelberg, and David Larson, as well as Marvin Fisher from Arizona State University, for their help. A generous research grant from Cleveland State University greatly facilitated this study in the early stages.

The portion of Chapter 7 dealing with Cheever appeared in slightly different form as "Closure in Modern Fiction: Cheever's 'Enormous Room' and 'Artemis, the Honest Well Digger'" in *Modern Fiction Studies*, Vol. 28, No. 1, Spring 1982, copyright Purdue Research Foundation. Reprinted with permission.

The material on James in Chapter 4 appeared under the title "Closure in Henry James's Short Fiction" in *The Journal of Narrative Technique*, Vol. 14, No. 1, Winter 1984. Reprinted with permission.

Permission to quote portions of John Cheever's "Artemis, the Honest Well Digger" from *The Stories of John Cheever* © 1978 by John Cheever was granted by Alfred A. Knopf, Inc.

Toward the End

Purpose, Methods, and Limits

When I first began to write short stories, I was rarely comfortable with endings. After submitting these stories to quarterlies and journals, I was even less confident; following an editor's occasional generous comment came the inevitable "was among the final twenty we considered—the ending was just a little flat for my taste," or "really had me charmed—until the conclusion, which I felt failed to fulfill the promise of the rest of the story." Clearly I needed to learn the magical technique of ending before I could thoroughly charm an editor.

I looked more carefully at the endings of well-known stories and began reading about endings. Few writers of "how-to" books commented on the problem, except for critics after the turn of the century who were willing to comment on anything, and even they were unsettled by the prospect of conclusion. J. Berg Esenwein, billed as "Sometime Editor of Lippincott's Magazine," in a book that ran through eight editions from 1908 to 1928, commented: "No one can give helpful counsel here. Use your own judgment. When you are through, stop; but do your best to conclude with words of distinction."[1] Others, too, had noted the problem; the Russian formalist, Boris M. Eichenbaum, writing about O. Henry, argued for the importance of the ending to a short story: "By its very essence, the story, just as the anecdote, amasses its whole weight toward the ending. Like a bomb dropped from an airplane, it must speed downward so as to strike with its warhead full-force on the target."[2] I was not sure I wanted my stories contributing to an arms race, but at least I knew I was not the first to be preoccupied with ending short stories.

Soon I came to the source: Edgar Allan Poe's 1842 review of Nathaniel Hawthorne's *Twice-Told Tales,* the essay virtually everyone points to in every study of the short story. I had read the essay several times before but had never needed to assimilate the message and thus had not remembered it. What Poe said about the shortcomings of one of his contemporaries, John Neal, now seemed familiar: "In the higher requisites of composition, John Neal's magazine stories excel—I mean in vigor of thought, picturesque combination of incident, and so forth—but they ramble too much, and invariably break down just before coming to an end, as if the writer had received a sudden and irresistible summons to dinner, and thought it incumbent upon him to make a finish of his story before going."[3]

As I reviewed Poe's other essays, I could see the extent of his reliance on endings as a compositional tool. In "The Philosophy of Composition" he noted that the plot "must be elaborated to its denouement before anything be attempted with the pen," and only then could the writer give plot "its indispensable air of consequence, or causation, by making the incidents, and especially the tone at all points, tend to the development of the intention."[4] In the essay on Hawthorne, Poe had applied these theories to the short story. Short stories should be designed with a "single effect" in mind, with "no word written of which the tendency, direct or indirect, is not to the pre-established design." By implication, aiming precisely for the ending best allows the writer to achieve the required singleness. The resulting compression would allow the short story to achieve effects "unattainable" in the novel. All of these points have been frequently cited by subsequent critics.[5]

Listening to other writers and reading what others have said about writing, I realized how many writers worked as Poe had advised—even a modern such as Bernard Malamud, for instance, maintained that he usually wrote knowing "the last paragraph verbatim."[6] Reading short stories in the light of Poe's injunctions I began to see how anticipation of the ending was used to structure the whole, even when the stories did not aim for Poe's singleness. I could see a new sense in Poe's familiar critical dicta, and I could see their wide application. Stories began to fall into patterns based on how they were structured in relation to the ending, and it was clear that endings were linked to historical changes in the genre. The discovery of these patterns and their evolution became the focus of the book I decided to write—not the book of magical incantations for endings, a "how-to" book, and not even a book solely about endings, but an account of the relationship of ending to the structure and development of the short story as a genre.

The argument seemed best organized along historical lines. For the first half of the book I have stressed the effect that endings have had on structure in the nineteenth century in the context of short-story theory at that time. In the twentieth century, endings were identified with the way causality and narrative restricted fiction by falsifying its view of life, and at this point writers frequently strove to give the impression of lack of resolution. Here I have examined the way writers have manipulated the reader's expectation of closure to create new kinds of endings.

Despite my dependence on the historical approach, I do not follow it strictly. I have, for instance, included Edith Wharton's "Roman Fever" in the section on nineteenth-century surprise stories because I am more interested in types of stories than in the history of the short story or the work of a particular writer. (Dates of first publication have been provided after each story on which I comment in order to maintain a sense of chronology.) I have usually concentrated on only one or two stories by each author; Henry James and Ernest Hemingway are the only two more broadly reviewed. The stories are generally representative, but they are not meant to characterize all the techniques the writer has used to end or structure his stories.

By restricting my study to American examples I do not mean to suggest that the short story is purely an American genre—clearly it is international, and what I describe here could be applied to the European short story as well. I feature American works largely because of the limitations of my own background. The omission of Continental literature as a source for new techniques, however, is a matter of principle. There is no disputing Austin Wright's claim that a writer such as James Joyce was "more significantly related to the American movement, directly or indirectly, than such American forerunners as Crane, Dreiser or Miss Cather," but the more I have examined foreign influences, the less significant they seem to American story structure.[7] Sherwood Anderson, for example, had not read Chekhov during the time he was writing what were sometimes called Chekhovian stories.[8] Reading Chekhov seems to have confirmed tendencies already in place rather than to have inspired new ones. James had been influenced by Honoré de Balzac, Ivan Turgenev, Guy de Maupassant, and others, but even a story like "Paste" has been thoroughly naturalized. Hemingway was clearly influenced by Joyce and by Gustave Flaubert (through Ezra Pound), but American influences—Gertrude Stein (an American expatriate, at least), journalism (according to Charles Fenton), or Mark Twain and Stephen Crane (according to Philip Young)—are just as important.[9] Even when a writer copies directly from a foreign source the result does not always reflect the assimilation of foreign techniques. When H. C. Bunner, a writer of short stories and society verse and editor of the satirical magazine *Puck,* adapted Maupassant's "The Umbrella" for his own "The Pettibone 'Brolly," he normalized Maupassant.[10]

Maupassant's story is a compact vignette; he reveals the pettiness of Mme Oreille by carefully limiting the situation to her miserly attempt to have the insurance company pay for the recovering of her husband's umbrella and by scrupulously controlling the pace to extract the maximum impact of her command in the last line. When, having gotten carte blanche from the insurance company, she commands the umbrella maker to re-cover the umbrella with his best silk regardless of cost, the contrast between her miserliness and her sudden conspicuous consumption efficiently completes the story with a snap. Bunner doubles the length of the story and omits Mme Oreille's burning a large hole in the umbrella to clinch the need for repair; he introduces details of appearance and setting Maupassant carefully pared from the conventional mode of storytelling; and he spoils the final line by rounding off the story with a glimpse of Mrs. Pettibone rebuking her husband. Bunner's case, to be sure, is exaggerated, but the point is generally true: awareness of foreign models has not necessarily stimulated new techniques.

Although I sometimes focus on endings alone, I am generally more interested in the way anticipation of endings serves to structure a story as a whole and in the causes of changing views of closure. I have tried to keep the terminology I use as simple as possible so as not to obscure these interests. To distinguish between different kinds of endings, for example, I have proposed a number of terms—"direct," "indirect," "imagist," and "compressed"—none of which should be taken as absolute categories. Directness and indirectness, which have to do with the degree to which closure can be anticipated, are terms arranged on a sliding scale. They are not poles; direction and indirection are properties that any plot has in varying proportions as it moves toward its conclusion. Each direct story contains a bit of indirection, and each indirect story is at moments direct. Forms can also be combined into hybrids—a direct story might take on features of the compressed form, for example—a point I deal with in the second half of the book.

My terms and system of classification are means to an end. I am less concerned with the individuality of the forms than with a sense of an underlying narrative grid that I think each reader applies to any story and that every writer depends on the reader knowing. I have chosen not to describe this grid scientifically, after the fashion of the structuralists, because such a description would not help the reader feel how this narrative expectation operates. Instead, I hope that a sense of this fundamental pattern, created by closural signals, will emerge from my case study approach. By making the reader aware of what closure is and how closural signals work throughout a story, and by demonstrating the effect closure has had on the American short story, I hope to improve our understanding of stories of any country in any period.

CHAPTER 1

Antecedents

Signals of Closure

The short story blends the brevity and intensity of the lyric poem with the narrative traits (plot, character, and theme) of the novel, but it blends with a sacrifice: the brevity is not so brief, the intensity not so intense, and the novelistic luxury of multiple plot lines spanning broad vistas of time and space, as Henry James put it, by "prizes, pensions, husbands, wives, babies, millions, appended paragraphs and cheerful remarks," must be foregone. Novels, of course, are not obligated to such expansiveness; James himself, as Marianna Torgovnick has shown in *Closure in the Novel,* developed the "scenic ending," an enigmatic openness that forces the reader to reconsider various motifs in order to understand the ending.[1] But as a consequence of the sheer demands of memory and attention in the novel, one may lose sight of the possibility of ending at all. In the short story, as Poe argued, the writer can at least keep the reader in anticipation of the ending. Consequently, in Robert Louis Stevenson's words, the ending of a short story has a greater structural significance for the rest of the work: "The denouement of a long story is nothing; it is just a 'full close,' which you may approach and accompany as you please—it is a coda, not an essential member in the rhythm; but the body and

7

end of a short story is bone of the bone and blood of the blood of the beginning."[2]

The word most commonly used now to discuss endings is "closure." Barbara Smith, one of the first to use the word as a literary term, defines it in terms of coherence, completeness, and stability.[3] The term is not applied evaluatively. More closure is not better closure; the nature and degree of closure has no bearing on the quality of the work as a whole. Closure characterizes all literary works in varying degrees; it is a natural property of any art form that moves in time, revealing itself gradually. It is the signal that movement may stop, that nothing more will follow. The reader's reactions, both intellectual and emotional, may continue, but without further stimulus other than memory or rereading. How complete the sense of closure needs to be varies from one period to the next, from one writer to the next, from one story to the next. Despite this diversity, all short stories use at least one of five signals of closure: solution of the central problem, natural termination, completion of antithesis, manifestation of a moral, and encapsulation. Because of the large role of endings in the structure of the short story, their influence is readily detectable.

The short story as a genre shares each of these signals with poetry, the novel, and drama, though the central problem and the moral are particularly significant for the short story. The central problem is unique because short stories, more often than novels, tend to focus on only one problem—to strive, as Poe put it, for a single effect. Most commonly a character faces a problem or desires to reach a goal. Closure is achieved if he solves the problem or reaches the goal. The story would seem coherent, complete, and stable. Stability is, of course, a broad term, for it encompasses also the failure to solve a problem or to reach a goal, provided the author can convince the reader the problem is permanently imbalanced or the goal is permanently out of reach. Presented this way, the central problem or, as I shall usually designate it, the "problem," seems simple.

Few short stories, however, especially modern stories, reveal their problems directly. The problem might develop on increasingly abstract levels, or characters might be unwilling to accept the nature of a problem, suppressing it not only for themselves but for the reader as well. The writer might choose an oblique style of telling that nearly conceals the problem. A wide variety of devices are available to enrich what is basically a simple matter of problem and resolution.

Natural termination, which is not unique to the short story, is the completion of an action that has a predictable end. If the subject of a story is a character's entire life, death is the natural termination, except, of course, for first-person narratives. A character who dies puts a very final, complete, stable, though not necessarily coherent end to his story. Other forms of natural termination are less radical: sleep, for instance, provides a natural close, and certain activities, once begun, imply natural ends. If one goes on a visit or trip, a return at some point is implied. If children are left with a babysitter, presumably the parents will return. Closure at this level has an automatic and undeniable quality. It is commonly linked to the first level, the basic problem. If there are doubts about whether Herman Melville's Bartleby could withstand the demands of his superior to behave as a clerk should, there are none by the end. Bartleby ends curled in a ball, at rest with kings and counselors.

Certain mental states are associated with natural termination. Statements of bliss, satisfaction, or euphoria are terminal in their own right, even if divorced from problems and their solutions. No further movement is required for a character attaining nirvana. It does not matter if the bliss is ironic, if a character deludes himself—the presence of this form of natural termination will nevertheless close the story.

All of these natural terminators have played an important role in American short fiction. To gain absolute finality, early writers such as Melville used them to underline closure ob-

tained through the other modes. Later writers have needed it
to lend the air of finality to problems that seem to resist solutions.

The third signal I have designated completion of antithesis,
though antithesis is only one (the most common) of this type.
The concept is at its base a spatial one, though in the short
story, with its emphasis on mental life, space is often metaphorical. The mental equivalent of a character setting out on
an adventure is a character exploring a range of attitudes toward a subject. Antithetical markers of closure indicate that
boundaries have been established, so that new territory (in its
metaphorical sense) need not be explored. Circularity, a return
to any aspect of the beginning, through verbal or situational
echo, is one form of antithesis. More broadly defined, antithesis is any opposition, often characterized by irony, that indicates something has polarized into extremes. The rhetorical
figure of antithesis, as Roland Barthes has pointed out, is particularly stable.[4] Many of Aesop's fables end with an antithetical statement, one with epigrammatic force. Antithesis
suggests symmetry, balance, and the tightly bound tension of
a permanent opposition. I use the term in the broadest possible
sense, as a descriptor of the reader's awareness of the limits of
some aspect of a work, in space, in time, or in a character's
attitude. If the story passes from positive to negative or vice
versa, from down to up, if a character changes from hating to
loving something or someone, the movement from the extreme of one pole to the other carries what I term antithetical
force.

This principle of antithetical closure is related to the nature
of closure in the other arts and to perception in general. Before
we can sense that something is closed we must be able to judge
its boundaries, to feel that it will not move further in space and
time. There are some specific peculiarities of this idea in the
short story, however, as comparison to similar ideas in music
will show. Music uses the idea of circularity in the concept of

the return to the tonic, a movement that creates closure. But in order for the movement to have closural force, the melody must move from somewhere to somewhere over a specified field. According to Leonard Meyer, we expect all the parts of a tone series to be touched on.[5] In literature, closure can be created by an even fewer number of steps—we need only to see a single antithesis. One curiosity of the antithetical signal is that the space between the poles is insignificant—only the sense of polarity need be established to create the sense of story. This is why Aesop's stories, brief as they are, neverthe- less give us the sense of "storiness." To express the antithetical principle in a more general sense, our concept of wholes is not particularly dependent on the range of space, time, or emo- tional attitude being covered. If we move from one extreme to another, if nothing indicates additional oscillation, then the thing perceived is presumably whole. It does not matter how much ground has been traversed, how many events have been portrayed, how long the middle is, for these are not properly conditions of ending. Applied to literature, the implication is that middles are not crucial to our sense of story. The effec- tiveness of an ending will depend a good deal on our accep- tance of the inevitability of the ending, and that is the function of the middle, which, through its hesitations and qualifica- tions, involves us in the movement to the end—but endings do not depend on middles to be perceived as endings.

Antithesis, then, of all the signals for termination thus far discussed, is the most firmly anchored not just in narrative but in the act of perception. It is the most primitive yet also the most subtle of the signals, for it is easily varied. Contempo- rary authors have continued to experiment with just how slight the sense of antithesis need be to activate this signal, how minor a sense of change in a character's attitude need be to signal a close.

The fourth signal I have termed the manifestation of the moral. Narrowly defined, this signal is unique to the short story. The short story has many sources, one of which is the parable or exemplum. Short stories, that is, tales that were very brief, were once offered as illustrations of the ideas that cultures regarded as necessary for survival. Aesop's tales illustrate concepts, and the epigrammatic statement of the concept necessarily closes the tale.[6] After the story had revealed its moral, it was over.

Our sense of what constitutes a moral has greatly expanded since Aesop's time. More broadly defined, the moral has become the theme or character's (or reader's) self-realization. Each story, of course, has a theme, and I do not mean to consider the moral totally synonymous with the theme in that sense. When we are aware, however, that a story that up until the end (the end in the physical sense, the blank space that signals, if nothing else does, that the story is over) has been factual, without any obvious intent to make an abstract point, and either a character or the reader sees the more general significance, the conclusion we draw has an effect analogous to the moral in the exemplum tradition. The reader's perception that a theme has emerged can give a short story a sense of having closed. The novel customarily announces its theme clearly and advances and develops it symphonically—repeating, doubling, contrasting, breaking apart, and reassembling the theme; the short story, merely in showing it has a theme, sometimes comes to its end, the completion of its purpose, as if in merely revealing a leap from the particular to the general, the story has fulfilled its purpose and might cease.

The fifth signal is encapsulation, a coda that distances the reader from the story by altering the point of view or summarizing the passing of time. It was a common marker in the nineteenth century, but Malamud's "The Jewbird," a story about a talking bird named Schwartz, shows that it is still useful. Schwartz has flown into the lives of the Cohen family and then has been expelled by the father, who feels displaced by the bird. The story ends:

In the spring when the winter's snow had melted, the boy, moved by a memory, wandered in the neighborhood, looking for Schwartz. He found a dead black bird in a small lot near the river, his two wings broken, neck twisted, and both bird-eyes plucked clean.

"Who did it to you, Mr. Schwartz?" Maurie wept.

"Anti-Semeets," Edie said later.[7]

There are two jumps in time: the first is between the main body of the story and the quoted passage, and the second is between the last two passages of the quoted dialogue, that is, between Maurie's question to the bird and Edie's (Mrs. Cohen's) answer. Presumably Maurie has retold his story to his mother at a later time, and it is her phrase, a quotation from Schwartz, the Jewbird, which ends the story. The double encapsulation puts a pair of time boundaries around a story that up to this point had a more concentrated and continuous time frame. The encapsulation, though, is not the only terminator—it merely underlines the natural terminator (Schwartz is dead, though with typically modern technique we cannot be entirely sure that the bird Maurie found was in fact Schwartz), and the line "Anti-Semeets" reveals the ironic, antithetical theme of the story—the Cohens themselves (especially Mr. Cohen) are the real anti-Semites, for they have rejected the Jewbird.

These various levels of closure rarely operate in isolation. The problem level is usually combined with a natural terminator or an antithetical marker. In "A Women's Restaurant" (1977), a story by a contemporary writer, T. Coraghessan Boyle, the narrator's problem is implicit in the title—he is barred from entrance to a restaurant for women only. "Women go there to be in the company of other women," the narrator claims, "to sit in the tasteful rooms beneath the ancient revolving fans and the cool green of spilling plants, to cross or uncross their legs as they like, to chat, sip liqueurs, eat." His exclusion galls him, and he responds with a direct and forceful statement of his goal: "What goes on there, precisely, no man knows. I am a man. I am burning to find out."[8]

The problem is solved when he ultimately succeeds in getting in, so that the story closes at the first level. Success, however, does not come easily. He has been stopped at the entrance while simply trying to stroll in; he has tried to break in after hours; he has been bounced by two girls, one wearing a studded denim jacket with the collar turned up. He finally enters by going in drag. The restaurant is everything he hoped it would be: "There they were—women—chewing, drinking, digesting, chatting, giggling, crossing and uncrossing their legs. Shoes off, feet up. Smoking cigarettes, flashing silverware, tapping time to the music. Women among women. I bathed in their chatter, birdsong, the laughter like falling coils of hair. I lit a cigarette and grinned" (p. 95). The narrator's attitude at this point is close to natural termination—he is close to nirvana. But his position is not wholly stable. He is, after all, in disguise. His bliss turns out to be only the rise before the fall. Drunk on wine, he goes to the women's room, bladder aflame, and forgets to sit down. His relief inevitably draws attention to itself, he is caught, he is thrown in jail. Slowly the solution comes to him:

> The police have been uncooperative, antagonistic even. Malicious jokes, pranks, taunts, their sweating red faces fastened to the bars night and day. There has even been brutality. Oddly enough—perhaps as a reaction to their jibes—I have come to feel secure in these clothes. I was offered shirt, pants, socks, shoes, and I refused them. Of course, these things are getting somewhat gritty, my makeup is a fright, and my hair has lost its curl. And yet I defy them.
>
> In drag. I like the sound of it. I like the feel. And, as I say, I have plans. The next time I walk through those curtained doors at Grace & Rubie's there will be no dissimulation. I will stroll in and I will belong, an initiate, and I will sit back and absorb the

mystery of it, feed on honeydew and drink the milk of paradise. There are surgeons who can assure it.

After all, it is a women's restaurant. [Pp. 97–98.]

Antithesis works in this story on several levels to support closure obtained through problem resolution. First, the solution is antithetical in the sense that the narrator has solved the problem by becoming (more precisely, proposing to become) his opposite. Irony has antithetical force here, too, and there are several ironies, first that the narrator ought to be suffering the depths of embarrassment, spied on and mocked, but he is at the peak of self-assurance. The extreme gap between the significance of a character's situation and his own view of it produces an effect analogous to antithesis, and because it fixes into stability a range of possibilities, it has closural effect. Another set of ironies further intensifies the sense of antithesis. The narrator, having once lusted for women, will now lose his capacity for some of what animated him. The rooster can strut among the hens only at the cost of his roosterhood. Obsessed with his goal, he plans to reconstruct himself and denies his original motive. Such abstract irony is the equivalent of movement in space: having moved as far as he has in attitude and motivation, he has reached the limits of a known universe. There is nothing more that can happen to him in this context.

As I have portrayed closure so far, it seems a static concept. In the reader's experience it has a much more active aspect. One can feel closure approaching. The signals here, for instance, are the growing sense of affirmation that reveals itself in the syntax. The phrase "these things are getting somewhat gritty, my makeup is a fright, and my hair has lost its curl" reveals through word choice that mentally the narrator is already undergoing a sex change. And the sentence "There are surgeons who can assure it" leaves the reader with a judgment to make, a guess of his own to grasp the narrator's intent.

Endings are in one sense in the reader's head; the reader feels them, creates them.

There is an overlap between terminators in the short story and in the novel, but not complete identity. Curiously, one natural terminator that plays a large role in the novel has no place in the short story—marriage. Presumably tales of courtship are necessarily too extended to be the subject of short fiction, and thus this traditional terminator rarely occurs. On this topic, however, Alan Friedman notes that not all marriages create closure; marriage at the end of E. M. Forster's *A Room with a View* suggests openness. Friedman also notes that some signals, such as the conflagration at the end of Joseph Conrad's *Victory,* do not necessarily seal off all the issues.[9] The point is significant; thematic considerations may override closural signals. In the section on Hawthorne and in the second half of this study, when I describe openness, I will again raise the issue of the interplay of thematic and structural signals. In the nineteenth century, the focus of the first half of this study, these signals commonly have closural force without being overridden by other considerations. When the Baron from Poe's "Metzengerstein" (1832) is taken by the Berlifitzing stallion to his conflagration, "the whirlwind of chaotic fire" of his castle, all of the elements of the story come to a close; theme and structure converge.[10]

The topic of how closural signals work and how they can be combined could be extended into a study of its own. But my object is to concentrate primarily on the way the expectation of closure controls perception of a short story, and for this we need now to look at the two main modes of approaching the end, the direct and the indirect.

Direct and Indirect Form

The form that I have characterized as direct implies an uninterrupted series of steps from the beginning to the end, without the intrusion of tangential episodes. The expectation of resolution is kept constantly before the reader, and the resolution itself is certain, even if the pace of the approach varies. Since stories of this type often have two possible endings, the story may veer in one direction or the other. When obstacles appear, characters immediately attempt to overcome them. The presence of obstacles represents indirection, but the longer the character's interest in his object is maintained, or more commonly, increases, the more sharply we see and feel the need for an end. In the direct mode we constantly have the sense that in removing the obstacles we are approaching the ending. Seen in these terms, the direct mode is the objectification of the complex interworking of desire and reality. Rarely do we get what we want, especially what we most deeply want, merely by asking for it. The world is filled with impediments to our desires; we must often reshape or redefine the world about us to bring our desires to fruition, and the direct mode is the mirror of this way of looking at the world.

Boccaccio, Day III, Fifth Story—Zima

Boccaccio's story from *The Decameron* (1350) is a good example of the direct mode, good, that is, if we see the story as Zima's. Although the story is presented by Elisa to illustrate a specific moral—the need to be very careful when testing the wits of others, for the tester may find himself outwitted—the focal point is not the tester, Francesco, but the man he tests, Zima (the Dandy).

Francesco seeks Zima's prize possession, his horse. What goads Francesco into thinking that he might succeed is that he knows Zima has been eyeing Francesco's own prize possession—his wife. Once Zima is contacted and he outlines the terms under which he will accept Francesco's proposed trade, the story is Zima's. Zima proposes to grant Francesco the horse if Francesco will merely let Zima talk to his wife for a moment, with Francesco present but not close enough to hear the exchange. Francesco accepts. Zima makes his plea to her but discovers his first obstacle. The wife will not say a word. Zima realizes from her facial expressions that his appeal has moved her, and he concludes, correctly, that the stingy Francesco, unwilling to give Zima any satisfaction, has bidden her to remain silent. But Zima has his end in sight, and his wits do not fail him. He acts out the wife's response, complete with an appreciation of himself and a proposed signal to accommodate his desires, two towels hanging from the window when Francesco goes out of town. The speech remains in the direct mode because it proposes a way to remove the obstacle. Zima then turns the horse over to Francesco, grumbling that the terms of the bargain have not exactly been met. Seeing how little response he has gained from Francesco's wife, he maintains that he is sorry he ever entertained a notion for her. The point of view then shifts to the lady, who mulls over Zima's proposal and the fact that her husband will be out of town for six months and concludes that "it's better to do a thing and repent of it than to do nothing and regret it." Two towels appear at the window, she leads Zima to her chamber, and "although this was the first time, it was by no means the last."[11] Zima achieves his goal, his problem solved, and the story has snapped directly to its ending.

This story clearly demonstrates the singleness of effect that Poe claimed for the short story. It is not as rigidly single as a modern writer might have made it—there are incursions into the points of view of Francesco and his wife that could more skillfully have been implied without leaving Zima's point of view. But it is by no means a primitive, crude piece of storytelling. First, the problem is presented with a significant twist. Though a feminist might argue that the story is a cruel portrayal of medieval chauvinism, of the lowly status of women, every element suggests an awareness of the imbalance of this kind of horsetrading. Zima has proposed a chivalric exchange, a few words, not possession of the woman. His intent, to be sure, is possession, but it must be achieved through consent, through persuasion. And Francesco's cuckolding comes about in large measure through his greed, his desire to give virtually nothing in exchange. Boccaccio, as he inspires Zima to enact the lady's response, could be seen as diverting the reader's attention from the end, for surely the reader's pleasure is in seeing the ingenious possibilities Zima has opened for himself, his chance to mirror his desires, to praise himself, to control the lady's behavior exactly in conformance to his desire. Since he is for the duration of his skit the woman, she will be exactly as he wishes. The fullness of this section is in part a product of Zima's ability to seize the moment and turn it to his purposes. But if the passage seems expansive and indirect, the ultimate effect, in the terms that I have established, is still direct. Directness has built into it moments of delay and retardation, but as long as the delay underlines our sense of a character, his desires, and his goal, the total effect is best designated as direct.

This story of Boccaccio's works very much as Poe claimed a short story should, with the pieces more or less in place to achieve a single effect. His technique contrasts with that of his immediate successor, Chaucer, whose methods perfectly illustrate the other pole of end-oriented design, indirection.

Chaucer, "The Nun's Priest's Tale"

Chaucer, in a story such as "The Nun's Priest's Tale" (ca. 1390), is nothing if not indirect. As do all of these early stories, "The Nun's Priest's Tale" has its moral: "But ye that holden this tale a folye, / As of a fox, or of a cok and hen, / Taketh the moralite, good men." The reader should "taketh the fruyt and let the chaf be stille."[12] What fruit, though, should we extract? The reader has a choice. The moral may be that those who wink when they should see will never prosper, as Chaunticleer concludes at one point, proud that having once been fooled by

the fox's flattery, he does not succumb a second time. Or
perhaps the moral is that one should resist flattery in the first
place, not listen to foxes who praise one's singing the better to
grab one's neck. Or perhaps one should heed one's dreams and
not fly down to begin any day that starts with an evil dream,
or perhaps the moral is that one should not listen to wives who
argue that dreams are to be forgotten, purged with laxatives,
disregarded by males who consider themselves valorous.
Since the story does not yield up its moral easily, it seems not
to have a specific end. We may for a moment even entertain the
suspicion that the author's craftsmanship is defective. He had
the model of stories such as those of Boccaccio; perhaps he
could not, as I argued of Bunner in his adaptation of Maupassant, understand what he was copying.

Difficulties in determining fixed meanings, fixed points
from which to regard the story, extend beyond consideration
of the moral. Identifying the limits of the story is problemat-
ical, embedded as it is in a prologue about its teller, the Nun's
Priest, and in turn embedded into the whole of the *Canterbury
Tales*. And if we limit the story to the tale of Chaunticleer, that
story in turn contains other stories—first, a frame, a widow's
yard wherein strut Chaunticleer and Pertelote, and then their
tale proper, or more precisely their two tales, one about their
disagreement over the dream and the other about Chaunticleer's capture and release. The modes of the two tales are
quite different. The dream tale is argumentative, consisting of
alternating set speeches by Chaunticleer and Pertelote, into
which are embedded additional exempla by the two speakers.
The capture and release tale seems sufficient by itself, marked
by the antithesis of Chaunticleer outsmarting the fox who
moments earlier had outsmarted him. The two tales are linked
because the capture tale fulfills the issue discussed in the dream
tale.

The reader beginning his way through Chaucer's maze of
embedded tales is likely to sense that the storyteller is in no

hurry to come to an end, partly because the teller seems more eager to start new tales than to end old ones and partly because the pace within tales is so slow. After Pertelote hears of Chaunticleer's dream she proceeds on a dissertation more extensive than any woman, let alone chicken, might devise. We are subjected to a parody of learned discourse, and any reader impatient with Chaucer for not getting on with it has missed the fun. What clearly interests the narrator is not the proximity of the end but the pleasure of getting there, for which purpose the end is best withheld. What Chaucer glories in is the ironies that surround his disputatious chickens. The dream discussion, after all, is enacted in the widow's barnyard. The pleasure of perspective, not the elusive vanishing point of the ending, is the real goal. Nowhere is this point more striking than when Chaunticleer, having told an exemplum and having recognized himself as the embodiment of Homer's Hector, afflicted by an ominous dream of archetypal significance, announces that Pertelote's beauty has helped him overcome his dread, after which he leaps from his perch, clucks over a kernel of corn, and twenty times satisfies his roosterly obligations on her. Even during the height of his passion, Chaunticleer is still being glorified, described for his likeness to a grim lion.

Chaucer is no garrulous, primitive fellow, spoiling the clean, hard effects won by Boccaccio; he has simply chosen to work with another method, one in which verticality, simultaneous views of a moment, is more significant than the direct movement toward the clarification of an ending. Chaucer, as Charles Muscatine has explained, was not writing a fable that makes "true and solemn assertions about life as it tests truths and tries out solemnities"; Chaucer wished to show that multiple perspective was in itself a way of looking at life.[13] Chaucer chose not to attack the idea of closure by writing a single unclosed story but undermined its effects by assembling a brilliant array of stories, whose varieties of closure would forbid the reader from assuming a final resting spot.

In Chaucer's hands the indirect mode is exemplified in one of its extreme forms. The impulse behind it is pursued with the vigor of Scheherazade, as if one's life depended on avoiding the end. The mode is characterized by prolongation, by a multiplicity of effects that obscure our sense of the story's purpose, and often by self-consciousness about the storytelling process. The need to reach completion is by no means disregarded, for the effects that indirectness seeks to achieve are in part dependent on the reader's sense of a norm. Without the imminence of closural signals, the sense of openness would not exist. The impulse for indirection is inherent in any direct narrative, for the momentary sense of tangency is needed to obtain involvement and surprise, to weave character and theme into the movement of plot. Only when the elaboration becomes more noticeable than the direction of the movement are we properly in the indirect mode. And when in that mode, as I have argued earlier, we are usually aware of the potential for a much more direct telling lying beneath the elaboration. Indirection is not a total rejection of the linear requirement of narrative but an intensification of one of its features.

Chaucer is so dedicated to indirectness that Poe would no doubt have regarded him as unable to come to the point, to shape his tale. If Boccaccio has the end point clearly in sight, Chaucer has virtually obscured it. The impulse that drove Boccaccio is synonymous with the impulse that would show itself later as the dominant one in the short story. And as Henry Seidel Canby has argued, Chaucer's impulse, not Boccaccio's, shaped the subsequent telling of tales in English. This impulse was not identical to Chaucer's, for his interruption of the direct progress of the tale added much vivid characterization and appropriate thematic complexity. Most who imitated him lost the sense of the functions of his interruptions, and their allusions degenerated into pedantry. Much material was grafted onto the tale in the way of courtly manners and rhetorical language that obscured the clean line, the direct movement to the end, but without the functionality of Chaucer's interpolations. As Canby put it, "After Euphues had done its work, there were only two roads open for the Elizabethan novella: either growth into a more extensive plot which could digest the rhetoric and discoursing, or a sloughing away of plot altogether, to let the letters, the arguments, and the reflections stand each alone and for themselves."[14] The second road led to the essay. The drama, which often mined the same tales, also siphoned away interest from the short tale proper. So by the early nineteenth century, although there are isolated examples of brevity and singleness of purpose, no writer pursued these goals with any consistency, until Poe noticed that he and some of his countrymen had begun to do so and, in his eyes, had begun to create a new form.

CHAPTER 2

The Early
Nineteenth Century

The Shape of the Short Story

Poe was not overly generous to his contemporaries in his 1842 review of Hawthorne's *Twice-Told Tales:* his comment on John Neal I have cited in the preface; William Gilmore Simms's "Grayling: or Murder Will Out," for all its virtues, he complained, still "has some glaring defects"; Washington Irving's collection, *Tales of a Traveler,* contains "graceful and impressive narratives," but not one "can be commended as a whole." Only three writers—Hawthorne, Nathaniel Parker Willis, and Charles Webber—are exempted from criticism.[1] An examination of stories by three writers Poe mentions—Neal, Irving, and Willis—and of Poe's own "The Fall of the House of Usher," seen in the context of short-story theory of this period, reveals the grounds for his complaints, shows how control of endings gave writers a structural device to shape their stories, and thus clarifies how Poe gave the direct form, and the short story itself, its modern shape.

Neal, "Otter-Bag"

The least skillful of the writers Poe mentions is John Neal, and his weaknesses are immediately apparent from a glimpse

at the beginning and the ending of one of his stories. Neal's
"Otter-Bag, the Oneida Chief" (1829), begins: "Of twenty-
eight Indian tribes that inhabited South Carolina, in 1670,
when it began to be settled by whites, twentysix had entirely
disappeared in 1785, when the history of the state was published."[2] It ends:

> "Your very good health," said the major.
> "Your very good health," said I—
> And here we parted. [P. 286.]

Virtually anything might have happened in between. The
opening seems more appropriate to an essay; the two characters mentioned at the end are not even visible at the beginning.
The "here we parted" line depends on the simplest natural
termination, characters in effect walking offstage. Neal seems
to know nothing more than the simple stop, without the force
of completion or conclusion.

The story is told through multiple levels as complicated as
those of Chaucer's "Nun's Priest's Tale"; without an ending
clearly implied at the outset, without a goal, the telling wan-
ders. After long digressions about where the tale came from
and who has the authority to tell it, or any other tale about
Indians, the narrator settles on the version he heard from a
major in the revolutionary army. This tale falls into two parts,
one describing how Otter-Bag outwrestled and then abducted
a soldier named Jerry Smith, and the other how Otter-Bag,
then a scout for the American revolutionaries at Valley Forge
under Captain Rudolph, met his downfall. The two parts appear to be separate tales connected only by a common
character, the Indian scout. The second part comes to a climax
when Otter-Bag stumbles across British soldiers and is
wounded not only by them but also by the Americans, who
believe he has led them into a trap. Presumably with Otter-Bag
shot (he absorbs thirty-four bullets) the story might end, the

moral about the fate of the trustworthy Indian might be announced, and at least one portrait of the vanishing noble savage would have been drawn, meeting the condition of the opening. But Otter-Bag clings dearly to life, and the major adds a second level, a report of Otter-Bag's own interpretation of his shooting, then gives us a third version, his own, as filtered through conversations with others and his reflections on the matter over time. The major then reveals that he is the brother of Jerry Smith, the soldier whom Otter-Bag had out-wrestled in the first part of the tale, thereby further linking the first and second parts. The major tells more about Captain Rudolph's treatment of the Americans who had shot their noble Indian guide. In this insert, while Rudolph rebukes his soldiers, Otter-Bag resurrects himself with a "rude, convulsive agitation" and is about to deliver another speech. The primary narrator suddenly abandons the major and his tale: "I was not in the humor to hear the whole of the story repeated—with variations," he claims, and then the final three lines of the ending, their parting, are appended.

The tradition of a multilevel tale is an old one, certainly older than Chaucer, and is still put to good use, as any reader of William Faulkner's "That Evening Sun" or John Barth's "Lost in the Funhouse" or "Menelaiad" would attest. But the interruptions in Neal's tale create a comic undercutting at odds with the pathos of the tale of the martyred Indian. The awareness of fictionality which multiple levels induce is functional in Chaucer's tale as in those of Faulkner or Barth; it is not in Neal's.

One might simply conclude that Neal is an artless teller, unaware of the requirements of his craft, but his interruptions are so systematic that they seem pathological evidence of what now is an outdated theory about fiction, a theory centering primarily on the need for the illusion of veracity. Neal seems not to have conceived of a story as an imaginative construct with a shape of its own, for he constantly strives to verify the truth of incidents, adding narrators who will attest to the credibility of their reports, or at least assert that whether truthful or not, the idea is at least useful and instructive because it illustrates a moral. In his account of his craft in an essay called "Story-Telling," he presents himself mostly as a recounter of anecdotes from the frontier, of adventures with "every word true," presumably noteworthy as accurate records of picturesque incidents, not as skillfully constructed imitations. The value of fiction is determined by its relation to fact, not its internal coherence. Fiction is simply reality shaped to make a striking point. When Neal received a letter from a reader of the story who was related to Rudolph and who wished to quibble about dates and suggest that Neal should have told more about Rudolph, Neal responded, "Had I known more, I should have told more."[3]

Given the history of short fiction, Neal's theories and practice seem standard. From 1820 to 1840 the genre was diffuse, still showing its lineage of the beast fable, the exemplum, the sketch, the character study, and the essay. Its practitioners seemed uncertain of its precise form and use. In eighteenth-century England short tales had been primarily a vehicle of moral instruction, more an apologue than outright fiction. According to T. O. Beachcroft, "The art grows up in the form of a known narrator telling the story in his own person, vouching for its factual truth, and usually pointing a moral."[4] What these attributes suggest is not a concern about the idea of shortness for "short" stories, or any concern for shape and design, but rather a doubt about the idea of fictionality. The truth of incidents, their factuality, needs constant verification; consequently, a narrator must attest to the credibility of his report and assert that whether truthful or not, the story is at least useful and instructive because it illustrates a moral.

Irving, "The Story of the Young Italian"

Although Irving's "Story of the Young Italian" precedes Neal's, it approaches the ideal of proportion that Poe advances and has the ending more clearly in sight, as here in the match of the beginning: "I was born at Naples. My parents, though of noble rank, were limited in fortune, or rather, my father was ostentatious beyond his means, and expended so much on his palace, his equipage, and his retinue, that he was continually straitened in his pecuniary circumstances"[5] and the end: "You who have pitied my sufferings, who have poured the balm of sympathy into my wounds, do not shrink from my memory with abhorrence now that you know my story. Recollect, that when you read of my crime I shall have atoned for it with my blood" (p. 78).

The Italian identifies his story with his entire life, looking back to his birth and forward to his imminent death. The beginning and the ending thus are not established in their own rights. They are defined instead by the beginning and ending of a human existence. Even so, they mark an awareness of the need of the story to establish its limits, a sense for design and proportion superior to that of Neal and Simms.

Poe cited "The Story of the Young Italian" as one with weaknesses, but it does at least demonstrate a firm sense of closure, dominated by repetitions, reversals, and reenactments. It also follows a conventional chronological pattern, beginning with the earliest days of the protagonist. The climax comes appropriately near the end, and whatever the story's failings, closure is not one of them. The story is weakened by the condensation of too much time into too little space—the narrator's childhood, his falling in love, his brother's death, his difficulties during a separation from his beloved, and his revenge upon the perpetrator of these difficulties. It summarizes too much and shows too little.

Although Irving in one sense had no difficulty applying the concept of closure to direct the action of the story toward a single climactic point, he did not realize the extent to which he had to let the ending dominate not just the action but space and time as well. The general weakness of the story is Irving's lack of originality, his failure to realize that he was working in a mode that would, because of its brevity, offer special opportunities and make special demands. His tale is basically a condensed novel. To the contemporary reader the piece seems like a scenario or outline for a novel, and the final result demonstrates the limitations of condensation. Having expanded the time frame, Irving had to abbreviate the content; he had no time to develop individual scenes. Irving understood the need to end firmly, but he did not see that ends in short stories must be adapted to special purposes; the scope of an entire life, unless narrowed rigorously, provides too much material for fully convincing treatment.

Willis, "Mabel Wynne"

Nathaniel Willis had mastered the method of narrowing the scope of the work through control of the endpoint. That Willis should have advanced the short-story art may not seem immediately credible—he seems to be a sketcher, one more interested in fragments of real life than in fuller, artistic designs. In the appropriately titled *Dashes at Life with a Free Pencil,* Willis notes that he had acquired "a habit of dashing off for a magazine any chance view of life that turned up to him, and selling in fragmentary chapters what should have been kept together and moulded into a proportionate work of imagination."[6] On the basis of such comments we would not expect him to espouse advanced theories of fiction or a well-developed sense of structure, but his theories are earlier versions of arguments Henry James was to make forty years later. Willis excuses his haste by observing that "dramas of real life are seldom wound up," so that his hasty work took on more of the appearance of everyday life and less that of art.[7]

Some of his shorter fiction, "Mabel Wynne" (1845), for instance, is more carefully designed than his casual sense of purpose would suggest. Willis begins the story with a young, much admired lady about to accept one of her suitors, a device that does not suggest imminence of termination. She receives a strange note from a fellow who was once a chimney sweep and whose subsequent rise in life was inspired by a chance view of her as a child while he was carrying out his duties. This fellow is known to her now, but his status has greatly improved, and his origin has been entirely concealed from her. The sweep turns out to be one of the suitors and not the one she would have expected.

By beginning with the young lady's receipt of the former chimney sweep's letter, not at the beginning of the chimney sweep's story, Willis designs a tale both compressed and yet fully realized. All that keeps the story from seeming more modern is Willis's habit of chatty authorial underlining, as in the final sentence: "I think my story is told—if your imagination has filled up the interstices, that is to say" (p. 97), a comment which directly, if inappropriately, highlights what Irving had missed, the point which writers such as Hemingway later exploited productively: the imagination will fill up the interstices, and thus a short tale can imply a much longer one.

Poe, "The Fall of the House of Usher"

Poe praised Hawthorne for his structural soundness, but the clearest application of Poe's theories about endings can be found in his own work. A comparison of the beginning and ending passages of "The Fall of the House of Usher" (1839) reveals the differences between Poe and his contemporaries. The story begins:

> During the whole of a dull, dark, and soundless day in the autumn of the year, when the clouds hung oppressively low in the heavens, I had been passing alone, on horseback, through a singularly dreary tract of country; and at length found myself,

as the shades of evening drew on, within view of the melancholy House of Usher.[8]

and ends:

Suddenly there shot along the path a wild light, and I turned to see whence a gleam so unusual could have issued; for the vast house and its shadows were alone behind me. The radiance was that of the full, setting, and blood-red moon, which now shone vividly through that once barely-discernible fissure, of which I have before spoken as extending from the roof of the building, in a zigzag direction, to the base. While I gazed, this fissure rapidly widened—there came a fierce breath of the whirlwind—the entire orb of the satellite burst at once upon my sight—my brain reeled as I saw the mighty walls rushing asunder—there was a long tumultuous shouting sound like the voice of a thousand waters—and the deep and dank tarn at my feet closed sullenly and silently over the fragments of the "HOUSE OF USHER." [P. 417.]

Reversals dominate. What was dull and dark at the beginning is by the end a radiant gleam. What was soundless is a tumultuous shouting. Even the clouds seemed ready to fall in the beginning, and by the end, the house has crumbled and sunk. Inversion is only half the strategy; a return to the original darkness and silence with the imminence of a fall is the other half. The narrator, who rode up to the house in the opening passage, now rides away, leaving as he came, alone. Dankness and darkness again prevail as the tarn closes silently over the house. The two passages demonstrate the movement toward a polar opposition and a complete return to the opening state, thus firmly establishing a sense of closure. Death and annihilation are everywhere—Madeline and Roderick die, and their house is swallowed without a trace, as if the madness they represented had never existed.

According to Canby, Poe created the modern short story by shifting the emphasis to the climax.[9] Even so, the terminal passage is not the climax, nor does Poe achieve his effects, as the passage cited earlier from "The Philosophy of Composition" would seem to predict, by the use of plot.[10] Causal sequence, an expectation of event leading to event with undeniable connections, is not what Poe attempted. The narrator has come to alleviate the gloom of his childhood friend, Roderick Usher, a specific task but not one he undertakes with a specific method. The narrator watches and describes rather than acts. Rather than describing specific moments in order, which would tend to create a plot, the narrator presents Usher's way of spending time—his rhapsodizing, his painting—in summary. Only "The Haunted Palace" and a picture of a "rectangular vault or tunnel" (p. 405) are objectified. Usher's sister Madeline dies (not unexpectedly because she is described as "approaching dissolution" [pp. 403–4] when first seen), but the death comes suddenly, with Usher "abruptly" informing the narrator that the Lady Madeline "was no more" (p. 409). Poe evidently seeks the eerie effects of accident rather than causality. After Roderick and the narrator put Madeline in a vault in the basement, Poe resorts to summary: over the next week Roderick comes to feel increasingly oppressed. Only at this point does a sequence of events in anything other than a generalized time begin, and only now are we introduced to actions with an anticipated termination. Roderick appears in the room of the narrator, throws open one of the casements to reveal a night "glowing in the unnatural light" of a gaseous exhalation from the tarn, and then reads a romance to pass away the "terrible night" (p. 412). At this point something like a plot emerges, created by the sequence of events in the romance Roderick reads, coinciding with noises about the house that indicate the nocturnal stirring of the not-yet-dead Madeline. This sequence, however, occupies less than one-fourth of the text. For a writer who places such emphasis on singleness of effect and for whom the climax is so important, this would seem more than an oversight.

In the 1842 review, however, Poe specified "singleness of effect," not unity of plot. And the unity of effect is supplied by the uniform way the traditional elements of story—setting, character, action, and theme—are interrelated, specifically through the imminence of an ending. The description of the setting (the house) predicts collapse. Though the parts are magically adapted to one another, the individual stones are crumbling, and a crack runs through them. True, the house holds together with the "specious totality of old wood-work which has rotted for long years in some neglected vault, with no disturbance from the breath of the external air" (p. 400), but the narrator is that external air, and simultaneous with (though not in any rational sense caused by) his entrance the invisible rot will claim all it infests.

Roderick, too, with his "cadaverous" complexion, points toward dissolution. He is linked with the house not only by the association of names, the House of Usher referring to both the family and the mansion, but also by his appearance, his silken hair "of a more than web-like softness and tenuity" (p. 402) floating like gossamer about his face, similar to the fungi that hang in a "fine tangled web-work from the eaves" of the house (p. 400). Both Roderick and the house suffer an "extraordinary dilapidation" (p. 400), and each seems to have absorbed the other. Descriptions of Usher are expressed in terms customarily applied to buildings or objects in space— the "formation" of the nostril, the chin "finely moulded" (p. 401), the "expansion above the regions of the temple" (p. 402)—whereas the house is animated by its "vacant eye-like windows" (p. 397), the "sentience" Roderick attributes to the stones, and the "importunate and terrible influence" (p. 408) the mansion exerts over him. If Roderick is linked to the house the imminence of its collapse is the imminence of his. Even his past is pointed linearly toward the brink, for the family has always descended directly, never putting out "any enduring branch" (p. 399).

The basic elements of character, setting, and theme predict total dissolution from the outset. Ultimately, Madeline, clutching Roderick, brings him down; the house falls not by causal sequence but because everything else falls, because all the parts of the story are interlocked, and they all implicitly suggest termination.[11] The singleness of effect is by and large the singleness, even the identity, of all the elements of the fiction. The work is so permeated by the expectation of an ending, the movement toward closure, toward absolute obliteration, so dense and automatic to the modern reader that it may seem mechanical.

Restricting himself to a single point of view, Poe creates a story that is more truly direct than Boccaccio's tale of Zima, which loses some of its directness by skipping to the consciousness of the other characters. By abandoning plot as the chief structural device to bind elements of the story and relying instead on the mood of termination and on correspondences between the various elements, character and setting, Poe achieves a density and compression that allow him to create a fully realized "short" story and not, as with Irving's tale, a "shortened" story. He could create an ending that did not depend on the presentation of a beginning and chronological progression of events (a plot) toward the ending. In one sense his real innovation was the discovery that "beginnings," that is, the causes for the segment of the action that he was interested in, could be submerged, modified, and suppressed, so that only the sense of ending remained.

Poe's theories about the use of endings to structure a story do not seem to have been applied consciously by other writers until several decades later, in particular after Brander Matthews had popularized Poe's theories. Developed as rigidly as Poe proposed, endings would become straitjackets. Character and description would be so distorted to the needs of design that the genre would encourage only phantasmagoric effects such as Poe's. Applied more intuitively, after the fashion of Hawthorne, working carefully toward the ending of the story proved to be a unifying structural resource free of Poe's narrow thematic strictures.

Direct and Indirect Form

Hawthorne, "The Celestial Rail-road," "Mrs. Bullfrog," "Roger Malvin's Burial"

Hawthorne's stories and notebooks suggest that, like Poe, he aimed for unity and compression. The notebooks repeatedly depict a unique, singular situation—a minister wearing a veil, a scientist who wishes to remove a birthmark—which Hawthorne then turns into a tale. He did not convert this concern for brief and carefully rounded form, as Poe did, into a critical theory but seems to have been guided by an intuitive need for unity. Unlike Poe, he apparently did not believe the sense of singleness was unique to the short story, and he constructed his longer works with the same concern for firmly controlled design and economy. *The Scarlet Letter* in particular has been likened in its technique to a short story, and Hawthorne used the same device in each of his novels, the circular return to the opening setting or situation, which frequently unifies his short stories.[12] Like Poe, Hawthorne relied on endings to structure his works, achieving closure by readily identifiable means, constantly controlling the reader's anticipation of an approaching culmination.

His attempt to point toward the conclusion at times leads to mechanical storytelling, as in "The Celestial Rail-road" (1843). The ending to which he points in this adaptation of Bunyan's *Pilgrim's Progress* is the termination of the train ride in the Celestial City, a goal the passengers never actually reach, for the narrator's guide, Mr. Smooth-it-away, turns out to be the devil himself. The onward pressure of the story is maintained not only by the motion of the train and by the reader's awareness of corresponding signposts in Bunyan's book that also lead to the Celestial City but above all by the series of clues that suggest the mechanization of man's ancient journey and tribulations is pure delusion. The revelation that Smooth-it-away is the reverse of what he seems closes with antithesis, revealing the moral that contemporary industrialization cannot mechanize the painful pursuit of salvation. The ending is further marked by the pyrotechnics of flame, not on the same scale as a Poe conclusion but with similar effect—a smoke wreath issues from Mr. Smooth-it-away's mouth and nostrils, and "lurid flame" darts from his eyes.[13] "The Celestial Railroad" is not one of Hawthorne's best stories; its singleness of purpose and effect is if anything the sign of its weakness. It rides evenly on the track of its initial premise but in consequence sacrifices the depth achieved in stories concerned less with mankind's collective experience and more with the individual soul.

Occasionally Hawthorne errs in the other direction with an ending that will not stay on the track, and he fails in much the same way that Simms and Neal do. In "Mrs. Bullfrog" (1837) the coach in which Mr. Bullfrog is making his wedding journey overturns, and he finds himself not beside the angelic image he has wedded but next to a toothless, bald-headed termagant who has just bloodied the nose of the coach driver. She orders the coach righted, all fearfully obey, and then Mr. Bullfrog, who has turned his back from a scene he cannot believe, discovers his angel again, complete with glossy ringlets and pearly teeth. He hopes what he has witnessed is a bad dream, but the suspicion that at any moment in the future his "connubial bliss" may be marred by an appearance of the "gorgon" lingers (p. 135). Hawthorne's use of the expectation of an ending is as clear here as in any other story—from the beginning Hawthorne has told us that as a result of the incident which he is about to narrate, Mr. Bullfrog feared the wisdom of overlooking "minor objections" (p. 129) to one's spouse.

The weakness is ultimately in the resolution. Mrs. Bullfrog confesses freely that she is not the shrinking innocent he may have thought and that her marvelous physical attributes are an illusion. But what bothers him most—the description of a court case involving a breach of promise in which she was the jilted bride—is what brings him to his knees. The five thousand dollars she won as a settlement will establish his business. Learning this, he embraces her and repents, "Happy Bullfrog" (p. 137) that he now is. Though Mr. Bullfrog clearly deserved to be brought into line, the ending relies on our consent to the proposition that for some people, of whom Mr. Bullfrog is unfortunately one, greed is all-powerful, that a large sum of money can paper over discontents of any magnitude. The fears that Hawthorne has exposed, comical as they are, run too deep to be so easily explained away. The difficulty is not that closure fails to structure the tale but that thematic considerations fail to arrive at a similar resolution; the story can be read only as an amusing tale.

"Roger Malvin's Burial" (1832) better exemplifies how the expectation of an ending involves readers in the action and evaluation of the characters and how potential thematic difficulties can in part be resolved to bind the story together. Comparison of the story's beginning and ending shows how close Hawthorne was to Poe's own practice. After a paragraph of introduction, providing historical background, the story proper opens:

> The early sunbeams hovered cheerfully upon the tree-tops, beneath which two weary and wounded men had stretched their limbs the night before. Their bed of withered oak leaves was strewn upon the small level space, at the foot of a rock, situated near the summit of one of the gentle swells, by which the face of the country is there diversified. The mass of granite, rearing its smooth, flat surface, fifteen or twenty feet above

their heads, was not unlike a gigantic grave-stone, upon which the veins seemed to form an inscription in forgotten characters. On a tract of several acres around this rock, oaks and other hard-wood trees had supplied the place of the pines, which were the usual growth of the land; and a young and vigorous sapling stood close beside the travellers.

The severe wound of the elder man had probably deprived him of sleep; for, so soon as the first ray of sunshine rested on the top of the highest tree, he reared himself painfully from his recumbent posture, and sat erect. [P. 338.]

The ending reads:

"This broad rock is the grave-stone of your near kindred, Dorcas," said her husband. "Your tears fall at once over your father and your son."

She heard him not. With one wild shriek, that seemed to force its way from the sufferer's inmost soul, she sank insensible by the side of her dead boy. At that moment, the withered topmost bough of the oak loosened itself in the stilly air, and fell in soft, light fragments upon the rock, upon the leaves, upon Reuben, upon his wife and child, and upon Roger Malvin's bones. Then Reuben's heart was stricken, and the tears gushed out like water from a rock. The vow that the wounded youth had made, the blighted man came to redeem. His sin was expiated, the curse was gone from him; and, in the hour, when he had shed blood dearer to him than his own, a prayer, the first for years, went up to Heaven from the lips of Reuben Bourne. [P. 360.]

Although the match of the two passages does not suggest, as with Poe, that the writer while composing the beginning has in hand a copy of the ending, turning it upside down to create the beginning, the end nevertheless clearly fulfills the beginning. The gravestone rock marks the same location; the sapling mentioned in the beginning is the one whose topmost bough falls in the end. Hawthorne further links the beginning and ending by treating them as virtually the only two fully dramatized scenes. Eighteen years separate the incidents, but only one other scene is provided, Reuben awakening from the swoon induced by his wounds. The time between passes in summary.

Like Poe, Hawthorne begins in a terminal mood. Even though "early sunbeams" rise, and even though Roger Malvin sits erect, both signals of commencement, markers of termination nevertheless abound—the weariness, the withered leaves, and the implications of the deprivation of sleep and the wound. A modern writer might have started closer to the actual end by beginning on the day Reuben shoots Cyrus and bringing in the first episode by flashback. Both devices, the more modern technique as well as Hawthorne's, give the illusion of compression.

Once past the brief, summarized middle section (covering eighteen years), a steady progression identifies the story as primarily in the direct mode. Parallels between this scene and the opening of the story continuously emerge: the time of year is the same, the scene (the forest) is the same, Dorcas praises Reuben for his charity eighteen years earlier, underscoring in effect Reuben's guilt. Reuben himself is agitated, nervous with the sense of expectation. And then with a stroke that might at first seem a contradiction of direct purpose but which in fact reveals the root relationship between direct and indirect, Hawthorne, at the point he has slowed down the action—has had Reuben fire a shot, then discover the gravestone rock, the sapling, but not yet know the consequence of his shot—skips back slightly in time and shifts to Dorcas's point of view. She has just fashioned a picnic spot, concluding with her durable optimism that the gunshot foretells an evening meal. Through her eyes the reader discovers the ghastly, pale Reuben rigid above the body of his son. Hawthorne's backward movement as he approaches the resolution is indirect only in the sense that the direct mode naturally incorporates some indirection, particularly near the ending. Once suspense has been relieved, closure is achieved by natural termination (Cyrus's death), by suggestions of downward movement (the descending withered bough) and above all by the release, the clarification that Reuben experiences.

Despite the convergence of closural signals, the ending has not always impressed twentieth-century critics, and the controversy on the subject reveals how disparities between thematic and closural features may function. Richard P. Adams, the first critic to notice problems with the ending, commented that "logically this ending makes no sense—indeed it makes badly perverted nonsense," though conceding that "psychologically it has some interesting meanings." The killing of his son Cyrus to pay off what Adams terms Reuben's "crisis of adolescence" must "make any reader feel uncomfortable."[14] Dieter Schulz and Sheldon W. Liebman have argued that Reuben's release is self-deception; Frederick Crews starts where Adams finishes, questioning first how we could "take seriously the religious notion that a man can make his peace with the Christian God by shooting his innocent son," then arguing that Reuben "feels guilty, not for anything he has done, but for thoughts of happiness—a happiness that will be bought at the price of a man's life." Reuben in effect stalks his son at the end, slaying him to release guilt that he feels in himself.[15]

If "Mrs. Bullfrog" is undercut by the ending and the reader is unable to view the story alternatively, a reading of "Roger Malvin's Burial" is deepened by an awareness of the ironic cost of Reuben's expiation. Whether or not Reuben understands the significance of the killing, the outcome is tragic, and the lie has extracted terrible consequences. Reuben is left without what he values most. There is, of course, a considerable difference in one's feelings about the nature of the tragedy, depending on whether one believes Reuben's self-deception ends at the point of killing his son or not even after that. The story

demonstrates not only the way in which the tone and proportion of the parts were shaped by the anticipation of the ending—how the introductory terminal mood, the foreshortening of the middle, the suspenseful movement toward
revelation, and the step-by-step sense of enclosing circularity
bind the story together—but also that the conclusion, however
closed it may appear on formal grounds, still forces the reader
to evaluate the thematic connections between the original
problem, the development, and the resolution. The harshness
of the penalty exacted will lead the reader to explore the psychological and religious ground of the story and to arrive at an
assessment of the significance of Bourne's repentance.
Whereas a twentieth-century writer might have used an incomplete action to force the reader back into the work to
resolve an issue thematically left open, Hawthorne in nineteenth-century fashion uses a close which while terminal still
forces further evaluation.

Irving, "Rip Van Winkle"

For many writers direct form is too constricting even when
loosened by the sort of thematic disjunction that Hawthorne
used in "Roger Malvin's Burial." The indirect form offers
more freedom from the requirement for tight structure, the
need for terminal convergence and resolution. Like the direct
form, it is an extension of the old-fashioned tale, but unlike the
direct pattern it retains the leisurely introduction and the broad
time span of its ancestor. The teller, slowing down the progress
of the tale with interpolations, announces his presence. The
indirect mode usually seems "plotless"—cause-and-effect
links between actions are weak, the story often seems to move
on tangents, on to new problems, and is marked above all by
delay and hesitation. It seems to share most of these charac-
teristics with a poorly shaped tale (Neal's "Otter-Bag" for
instance), but indirect fictions functionally and effectively

foreground hesitations and delays. An awareness of ending, and the reader's delay in reaching it, makes the fiction what it is.

"Rip Van Winkle" (1819), true to the pattern of the tale, begins with a leisurely descriptive passage unmarked by tension that might suggest future conflict. The Kaatskill mountains vary in their appearance according to the weather, but the alterations are rhythmic, predictable, and in all forms "magical."[16] As the focus narrows gradually to a specific person in the village, a problem is revealed. Rip is a henpecked husband who would like to escape his wife's harangues. Irving heightens the problem with metaphor—domestic tribulation is a "fiery furnace" (p. 30), but in context the metaphor is an exaggeration, the playful wit of a detached narrator. The narrator consistently presents Rip's problem in a context that undercuts it, describing Rip, for instance, as "a simple good natured man . . . a kind neighbor, and an obedient, henpecked husband" (pp. 29–30). The syntactical arrangement of the "henpecked husband" as an anomaly in the list may surprise, but it also levels the term to the same plane with the previous words, "kindliness" and "obedience." The narrator is even willing to argue that having a termagant for a wife can be an advantage, for it can teach the "virtues of patience and long suffering," so that such a wife could ultimately be a "tolerable blessing." (If so, Rip was "thrice blessed" [p. 30].) The rhetorical treatment undercuts our perception of the problem as an enduring discomfort, converting it to an occasion for the narrator's wit, and the pleasure is flowing with that rather than finding a solution. Instead of moving the plot forward the problem dissipates itself into irony.

Rip does not seem motivated to resolve his problem. He trudges repeatedly through the same situations—into the hills to shoot at squirrels and pigeons—activities best captured, as Irving has done, by summary rather than dramatic scene. The only development or intensification seems to be the result of a cycle: he continually neglects his domestic duties, which increases his wife's rage, which in turn intensifies his need to withdraw, a spiral that can only degenerate further. Throughout, Irving adopts stylistic strategies that embellish the theme rather than advance the plot. Analogies ("a sharp tongue is the only edged tool that grows keener with constant use" [p. 31]) predominate at the expense of action.

The break from this degenerating spiral occurs without apparent cause. One day Rip, wandering in the woods, heaves a sigh in expectation of returning to home and the "terrors of Dame Van Winkle" (p. 33). And then he hears his name called. Once he follows the squat old fellow with the keg on his shoulder, the story seems to diverge on a tangent. Rip experiences a shadowy ritual from the past which means nothing to him, though the reader attentive to details can infer something of the psychological significance of the scene. The passage through the cleft in the mountain into a hollow that forms an amphitheater suggests a womblike experience; the "party" taking place is a purely masculine event, which seems to have as its goal a total stupor analogous to Rip's withdrawal from his wife.

The significance of the journey is not particularly clear even in these terms. Rip seems to be passing from one version of the feminine—mundane, abusive, and demanding—to a more archetypal one, but in the womb he meets only a collection of dour little child-men who seem no more content with their lot than he is with his. Any explanation that the reader may construct to relate this part of the story to the first part is tenuous at best. To use the language of structuralism, the section might more accurately be described as paradigmatic rather than syntagmatic, that is, it adds vertical depth instead of advancing the horizontal action of the story.

Once Rip awakes, a second tangent begins, with two related parts, first the section dealing with Rip's slow realization that twenty years have passed, then the second, dealing with political ironies. In the first part the reader is likely to wonder when Rip will read the clues that reveal what has happened to him. The section comes to a climax that returns to Rip's initial problem, now transformed—he no longer has a needling wife; he no longer has anything: his house is "empty, forlorn and apparently abandoned. This desolateness overcame all his connubial fears—he called loudly for his wife and children—the lonely chambers rang for a moment with his voice, and then all again was silence" (pp. 36–37).

The second section advances by contrasting American manners to colonial manners, the bustle of the American present to the lethargy of the Dutch past. The story comes toward a close not on the issue of Rip's domestic intranquillity but on the question of who he now is. It is as if the bottom of the story had dropped out, and the first order of business is merely to reestablish who the characters are, not what the story is about or where it is headed. Rip finally grasps what has happened to him, asserts his identity, and has it confirmed by old Peter Vanderdonk. An explanation is offered for his meeting with the little old men in the wilderness—they are the ghosts of Hendrik Hudson and his crew—thus recalling the middle section of the story, in a sense incorporating it and binding it to the present. Closural signals now dominate. Rip resumes "old walks and habits" and finds many "former cronies," a circular return to the more stable elements of the beginning. Rip has progressed by wish fulfillment to something like nirvana, a terminating state; he has "arrived at that happy age when a man can be idle, with impunity," and he can now be "reverenced as one of the patriarchs of the village." The closing sentence recalls the opening reference to the landscape, brings the reader down to the present, encapsulating the tale, and suggests how the content of the tale has been condensed into a usable interpretation in the present. Even to this day the old Dutch inhabitants "never hear a thunder storm of a summer afternoon about the Kaatskill, but they say Hendrick Hudson and his crew are at their game of nine pins; and it is a common wish of all henpecked husbands in the neighborhood, when life hangs heavy on their hands, that they might have a quieting draught out of Rip Van Winkle's flagon" (p. 41). Only one item weakens closure, the remark that Rip's telling of the tale was noted to "vary on some points every time he told it," which suggests that what seemed factual may be Rip's fiction; stability is undermined by the implication of variation.

Assimilation of all the parts of the story to a single whole is not simple. One may relate the passages of political satire to Rip's domestic difficulties by arguing that each is about the escape from a form of tyranny, but this is association by analogy, not plot. The narrator seems to depend on capturing the reader's attention more by his wit and grace than by the suspense of sustained, connected action. Irving makes no attempt to disguise this trait; a story for him is "merely . . . a frame on which to stretch my materials," an occasion for the "play of thought, and sentiment, and language."[17] And yet the overall effect of the story is unlike that of "Otter-Bag." In Irving's story the mode and the subject are congruent; wish fulfillment by its nature is indirect. Rip would simply like to wake up one morning and find all his troubles gone—they are too complicated for him to do anything about himself, and direct action other than reforming his own character would be morally ambiguous. He could not, for instance, walk out on his family or take an ax to Dame Winkle without at least inner retribution. Rip's problem has magically been solved in a manner perfectly congruent with his pyschological needs.

The indirect mode, one in which things seem to happen gratuitously, is best suited to express wishes that can be realized only by short-circuiting the resistance of reality. The leisurely pace lulls away the connection between wish and fulfillment, between problem and resolution. Dame Winkle is done away with by the magic of time and is tucked away more firmly than any of Poe's shadowy brides, who are apt not to regard death as any bar to reunion with their lovers. Closural signals are just as firmly applied in the indirect mode, and though we do not appear to be moving toward the end, we certainly arrive there and realize we were going there all along and did not know it. In this sense the indirect mode is still end-directed, but the movement toward the end is largely concealed.

"Roger Malvin's Burial" and "Rip Van Winkle" are remarkably similar: both Rip and Hawthorne's Reuben have grown careless about their domestic responsibilities, and both have suffered adverse turns of fortune. Both are drawn by subconscious forces into the wilderness. Each has suffered, either literally or figuratively, from nearly twenty years of unawakened "sleep." Both seem to have been stuck in a critical rite of passage out of which they have not been able to pass. For Rip, emergence from this sleep is comic; for Reuben, tragic. The way the subconscious core erupts differentiates the two, and the way the author designs the subconscious to operate determines the appropriate storytelling mode. The reader of "Roger Malvin's Burial" is in a position somewhat analogous to that of Reuben's unconscious. The reader senses the logic and the pacing of inexorable purpose with which his unconscious manifests itself. Not until the final instant are the same actions so clearly purposeful to Reuben (many have argued, as we have seen, that he never understands). The reader of "Rip Van Winkle" is in Rip's conscious position. Everything looks indirect because that is how Rip sees his unconscious. Irving allows Rip's unconscious comically to reconcile the disparity between wish and reality by bending reality; Hawthorne, in contrast, has Reuben's unconscious bend Reuben. When the work of the unconscious is best achieved without the awareness of the ego (while the ego sleeps), the indirect mode is best; when the unconscious must bring the ego toward a reckoning, the direct mode is appropriate. In each case the ending dominates the structure of the tale but in strikingly different ways.

Melville, "Bartleby the Scrivener," "I and My Chimney"

No writer remains precisely at the same spot on the direct-indirect scale from story to story, though most tend to favor one mode or the other. Some, however, such as Herman Melville have ranged broadly: for example, "Bartleby the Scrivener," except for the opening, is basically direct; in "I and My Chimney," the indirect mode dominates.[18]

"Bartleby" is direct in the sense that it progresses step by step, with causal links in place, and from the beginning it reveals the terminal tonality that characterizes Hawthorne's and Poe's stories. Bartleby's encroachment on the lawyer and his staff, because of his "prefer not to" attitude, mounts steadily from incident to incident—from his initial "gorging" of documents to his first refusal to copy, through his refusal to run an errand, his occupation of the office over the weekend, his dead wall reveries, his "preferring not" to leave when dismissed, his refusal to leave the premises, which forces the rest of the office to move to new quarters, his expulsion to the Tombs (a prison), his death. Paralleling his actions are the responses of the narrator, at first a condescending user, then a piqued supervisor, then a condescending charity-giver, then himself momentarily an outcast, a melancholiac. Next he is a self-congratulating disposer of Bartleby, then a man who discovers he is yet his brother's keeper, and ultimately a man moved, at least to some degree, to a sense of understanding and pity. Although the extent of his understanding has been debated, and therefore the extent of his change, he has undergone a lengthy and seemingly complete catalog of responses to Bartleby. The use of the natural terminator, death, and the thorough exhausting of attitudes, the inversions of roles (at

times Bartleby seems more the master than does the narrator-
lawyer) all contribute to a firm sense of closure. All the variations
and hesitations seem to narrow themselves down resolutely,
each one more so than the last, to the ultimate conclusion.

The tonality of termination is subtly conveyed in the sense
that the opening seems terminal more in retrospect than as first
read. Bartleby, when he first appears, is a "motionless young
man," one "pallidly neat, pitiably respectable, incurably forlorn," one soon seen as "cadaverous."[19] At the time the narrator's description seems only fancifully metaphoric, but by
the end, Bartleby is literally motionless, literally pallid, literally a cadaver. In a sense, Melville has taken the machinery of
Poe-esque gothic, creating a walking cadaver who ends in the
Tombs, superimposing this aspect of the story as a metaphoric
level above a very human and socially identifiable type, the sad
fellow who once clerked in a dead-letter office. (The idea of
seeing this story as an echo of Poe's is not altogether fanciful—
at one point the narrator thinks of masoning Bartleby into the
walls to get rid of him, demonstrating through that allusion
the narrator's awareness of Poe.) Melville exhibits a firm control of the elements of design (if we can forgive him his leisurely talelike opening) and proceeds in the direct mode which
Poe and Hawthorne had established before him. As in "Roger
Malvin's Burial," internal discrepancies (in this case created
partly by the narrator's inability to understand completely
what he has seen and partly by his open admission of puzzle-
ment over Bartleby) give the story its "ragged edges," as
Melville was later to say of truth in *Billy Budd,* but the form as
a whole is carefully symmetrical, converging and consuming
further actions. Thematic openness is not supported by structural disjunction.

The story "I and My Chimney" (1856) has an identifiable
problem—the narrator wishes to resist the possibility of having his chimney razed—but Melville is even slower getting to
the problem than in "Bartleby." The opening, after the fashion

of Irving, is dominated by wit focused on two gray-headed old smokers, the narrator and his chimney. What interests Melville is clearly an analogy, not an action. He has picked a spatial rather than a temporal topic and is taken up with modifying our sense of this object, with its crevices, its closets, its flues, its possible secret chambers, both as a literal and a metaphoric object. The chimney becomes variously a plant, a belfry, a pyramid, a whale, a royal personage, a Druidical forest; it is a political philosophy, a phallic symbol; it is the narrator himself. Had his wife succeeded in having a passageway carved through the chimney to the dining room, the narrator concedes, "some Belzoni or other might have succeeded in future ages in penetrating through the masonry, and actually emerging into the dining-room, and once there, it would have been inhospitable treatment of such a traveler to have denied him a recruiting meal" (p. 173). By metaphor, space in the story is transformed into something much greater than a physical dimension. The chimney is a subject for vertical elaboration, not for the horizontal development of plot and the sense of directness.

Above all, the narrator does not want change. His desire to maintain the status quo is the backbone of all the indirection. Once the narrator gets his certificate from Mr. Scribe, an architect whom the narrator thinks is in collusion with his wife—a certificate indicating that there are in fact no secret chambers, so that his wife must keep her bargain and stop trying to bring the chimney down—the story may end, though not without some fine encapsulating touches. Articles deprecating his chimney appear in the village paper, anonymous letters arrive, another architectural reformer appears, but worst of all he once found "three savages, in blue jean overalls" commencing an attack on his chimney, nearly braining him with removed bricks. But he and his chimney, as he claims in the final line, "will never surrender" (p. 189). The story is a playful (though in some ways for the narrator also painful) exercise in indirection, a tantalizing exercise in multiple meanings. It is not without parallel to the other great indirect story of the period, "Rip Van Winkle," another story of domestic tribulation, another tale of a moss-grown old man, who, if less blessed than Rip by his final resolution, has held out for his independence against an encroaching Americanism, a projecting wife who values only the new. The end, which threatens to be a final, inevitable encroachment, is held at bay; the indirect mode is particularly appropriate as a vehicle for a situation in which termination is not desired.

CHAPTER 3

The Later
Nineteenth Century

Conventional Patterns

The impact of Poe's argument about the significance of endings on his contemporaries was minimal. Even writers who borrowed directly from him seemed to imitate his subjects or style, not his structural innovations. Fitz-James O'Brien, in a story such as "The Diamond Lens" (1858), the subject of which is the pursuit of a 140-carat diamond required to build the ultimate microscope, betrays a clear debt to the diction and content of Poe's ratiocinative suspense tales, but the turns the story takes—after carefully concealing a murder to get the diamond, the narrator falls in love with an animalcule he sees in his microscope, a creature that dies pathetically as her water dries up, after which the grief-stricken narrator becomes a mad lecturer—spoil any singleness of purpose. In the later part of the century (the publication of Brander Matthews's *Philosophy of the Short-Story,* first in *Lippincott's Magazine* in 1884, and then as an expanded monograph in 1885, serves as a convenient identification point) the consequences of Poe's theories for short fiction were more widely recognized, largely in order to combat the continuing formlessness of the genre.

Many writers of the period were no more concerned with the uniqueness of short fiction, let alone the function of the ending in establishing that uniqueness, than Simms or Neal. Short stories frequently resembled condensed novels, covering a long span of events without developing any dramatized scenes. Writers working in this mode did not provide a formal justification; their approach seems a consequence of a lack of theoretical reflection rather than a conscious decision. From time to time there were appeals for the uniqueness of short fiction—in 1869, an anonymous article in *Appleton's Journal* argued that a short story had "one definite idea thrown into a compact, symmetrical form," and in 1898 Frederick Wedmore argued that the short story was not "'a novel in a nutshell,'" that it could not "possibly be a *precis,* a synopsis, a *scenario,* as it were, of a novel"—but these were pleas against what was in effect the common practice.[1]

Page, "Marse Chan"

Stories such as Thomas Nelson Page's well-known "Marse Chan" (1884), a prime piece of southern antebellum local color, sometimes contain the kernel of the short-story form proper. After the fashion of Neal or Simms, Page establishes a frame, but unlike theirs a cleverly designed one that a later writer might have turned into a short story in its own right. The narrator of the frame overhears Sam, a former slave, addressing an "old orange and white setter, gray with age, and corpulent with excessive feeding" that has sauntered up to a fence and awaits Sam's help.[2] Sam declares: "Now, I got to pull down de gap, I s'pose! Yo' so sp'ilt yo' kyahn hardly walk. Jes' ez able to git over it as I is! Jes' like white folks—think 'cuz you's white and I's black, I got to wait on yo' all de time. Ne'm mine, I ain' gwi' do it!" (p. 169). Sam pulls down the fence for the dog anyway. Even if the rest of the story shows that Page has little sense of structural singleness, the frame shows that he does have a well-developed sense of effect, the lump in the throat called up by the muted sense of the ravages of time and heroic self-sacrifice, by the thought of a slave who while denouncing this canine substitute for his master is nevertheless moved to show his unending loyalty. Another scene with the dog serves to close the story as well: Sam calls out to his wife, asking whether the dog has reached home. Between the framing incidents is an expansive history of Marse Chan (Master Channing) himself, his birth (Sam, eight years older, was called upon to hold him and serve him for the rest of his master's life), Channing's protective feelings toward Annie (the daughter of a neighboring plantation owner), the subsequent falling out of the two families because of politics, a duel with Annie's father in which Channing spares the father, Annie's rejection of her lover's marriage proposal because the honor of the family has been tarnished by the duel, Channing's enlistment in the Civil War, and finally, Annie's change of heart. Channing, energized by her letter, heroically leads a military charge—and dies. Page, with a clear sense of design, brings the story to a climax with this striking irony and rounds off the tale with Sam carrying Marse Chan in his arms, thus recalling the time Sam held his master as a newborn. Expectation of termination does not, however, control the reader's progress through this nineteenth-century soap opera, either positively, as in the direct mode, or antithetically, as in the indirect. The story is primarily episodic, in the tradition of the chivalric romance, filled with high ideals and heroic behavior, and the reader's attention focuses on the capricious reversals of fortune that afflict Marse Chan, not on anything like an endpoint.

The Surprise Ending: Aldrich, O. Henry

If tales written as condensed novels rely too little on endings, stories with surprise endings rely on them too much. Though surprise endings are not, as a 1930 dissertation by Graves Glenwood Clark has shown, numerically dominant in the whole of any writer's work until O. Henry, the effect of surprise endings on short-story structure and on the popularity of the form extended beyond the actual number of examples.[3] Writers' careers were established by such stories. The reputation of Thomas Bailey Aldrich, who became an editor of the *Atlantic Monthly*, was made by his 1873 story "Marjorie Daw," the title piece in his first collection of short fiction, a story frequently reprinted in anthologies of the time and still the only story specifically identified in the *Oxford Companion to American Literature* citation for Aldrich. Frank Stockton's "The Lady or the Tiger" (1882), a sensation when it first appeared, was turned into an operetta, and its fame helped to establish Stockton as a writer; the story is still frequently reprinted in high school anthologies. Of the six stories Frank Luther Mott cites in *A History Of American Magazines* as the most widely known of the second half of the nineteenth century, three have surprise endings: "Marjorie Daw" and "The Lady or the Tiger," as well as another Aldrich story, "Mademoiselle Olympe Zabriski."[4]

Clark classifies surprise endings into seven different categories, a system too extensive and cumbersome for use here.[5] These categories reduce to the single notion of concealing from the reader until the end a fact that would have entirely changed the story. Often the missing fact is trivial, for instance, that a dog whose name suggests immensity was small (Aldrich's "Goliath"). In one such story, the reader discovers at the end that a lion bit off the head of its trainer because an acrobat jealous of his wife's attention to the lion's trainer put snuff in the trainer's hair, causing the lion to sneeze and clamp his jaws shut at a particularly inopportune moment. In Frederick Perkins's *Devil Puzzlers,* the devil at the last moment loses his Faustian bargain with a certain Dr. Hicok because Mrs. Hicok poses the devil an insoluble question: she gives him one of her stylish new hats and asks which is the front. In Nathaniel Willis's early example of the form, "Kate Crediford"

(1845), a man goes to the performance of an actress with whom he was once in love and finds himself once again attracted to her. She displays in her performance the touching air of pensiveness and melancholy that he once thought she lacked and which had once led him to abandon her. His love rekindled by what he has seen, he writes passionately, requesting permission to see her, and in the closing incident in the story receives a letter, not from her but from her husband, explaining that she is now married and that her unhappy expression during the performance was the result of having eaten "an imprudent quantity of unripe fruit."[6] "Marjorie Daw" is an extreme example of the pattern: the title character, the reader discovers at the end, never existed—she was the creation of a young attorney trying to amuse a friend who had slipped on a lemon peel, broken his leg, and was confined for the summer in his New York apartment, strapped into his bed with "the hot weather turned on."[7]

The facts that customarily constitute the revelation of a surprise story, from Aldrich's tiny Goliath, to Willis's unripe fruit, and to Aldrich's nonexistent heroine, are invariably out of proportion to the stir they create. Presumably the shock of the ending is intensified by the gap between what the reader has expected and what he finds, but such a device exposes the writer to "reader backlash," resentment at having been taken in. Perhaps one might learn something by reexamining the way a writer has tricked the reader; a reexamination of Ambrose Bierce's "Occurrence at Owl Creek Bridge" might show the reader how he was deluded into believing Peyton Farquhar had escaped the union guards, but the reader is unlikely to derive more satisfaction than that.[8]

Readers are not likely to reread a surprise story. As Edmund O'Brien pointed out, the defect of the surprise story is that "it can never give pleasure in the same short story twice."[9] A second reading could serve only to show whether the writer had played fairly with the reader's expectations. In this respect, surprise endings distort the end domination that Poe proposed. If John Neal weakened his story by failing to work carefully toward the end, writers such as Aldrich and Bunner weaken theirs by working too carefully, enlarging the significance of the end so that the beginning and middle shrink disproportionately. When a story elaborates a beginning and middle solely to increase the snap of the ending, as does Aldrich's "Mademoiselle Olympe Zabriski"—with its careful attention to the curiosity of all the protagonist's club members as to what could be affecting him and with his mother's visit, during which she threatens him with loss of inheritance should he continue to pursue an actress—the effect of the ending, the revelation that the mademoiselle is in fact a boy, is likely to seem so contrived that the reader will feel manipulated. Too much of the reader's attention and energy has been directed solely toward the final effect. The longer such a story goes on, the more the sin is compounded.

Singleness for Poe meant unity, wholeness, and interrelation of all the parts, not one effect exalted above all others. The singleness of pure surprise endings returns the short story to one of its sources, the anecdote, a form in which the beginning and middle are elaborated solely to enhance the effect of the "snapper," the punch line, at the end, an effect particularly obvious in O. Henry's stories. "A Lickpenny Lover" (1908)—a story about a dime-store girl who turns down a rich lover's offer to take her to a place with "grand and lovely palaces and towers full of beautiful pictures and statues," a city where all the streets are water, because she thought he wanted to take her to Coney Island—can work only if characters are minimized to stereotypes.[10] The girl must be a thoroughly brainless shopgirl, the man a rich dilettante. O. Henry is masterful in making the stereotypes come alive in dialogue, but he cannot allow either character to take on any roundness that would distract us from the economy and efficiency of the final joke about the girl's misunderstanding.

Poe, "Ligeia"

Poe's stories contain surprise and shock—elements that are requisites for the climactic effects—but surprise and shock are carefully prepared for and carefully integrated into the whole of the story. At the end of "Ligeia" (1838), the narrator beholds a shrouded figure advancing "bodily and palpably" (p. 329) into his apartment and knows it is surely not "the fair-haired, the blue-eyed Lady Rowena Trevanion of Tremaine" (p. 330). The "ghastly cerements" fall, revealing hair "blacker than the raven wings of the midnight," and the narrator shrieks the final line, with all its hesitations and repetitions for maximum force: "Can I never—can I never be mistaken—there are the full, the black, and the wild eyes—of my lost love—of the Lady—of the LADY LIGEIA." The transformation is hardly a complete surprise, for all the details of the story to this point suggest, as they should according to Poe's theories, that the narrator's first wife, Ligeia, has the desire and power to transcend death and replace the second wife. The surprise has two additional components separate from the surprise that characterizes the assimilation of new information. One component is the shock of discovering that the laws of nature have been suspended, a shock made more credible by the narrator's careful evocation of mundane details. The transformation of the corpse was inevitable but still a surprise because we do not expect the laws of nature to be suspended. The second component is especially necessary to the lasting effect and the significance of the story. Subconsciously the narrator wants Ligeia to return, yet morally her reappearance is compromised by the unnaturalness of co-opting the life of another being. This moral contradiction directly touches a sensitive nerve: our suspicion that our deepest wish for the permanence of our love may spring at us at an ultimate cost, the obverse of all we had hoped for. We are surprised to see an open formulation of a connection between desire and dread that most of us would rather leave unstated. Surprise in Poe is not assimilation of trivial facts—it is the baring of deepest and most feared yet desired emotions.

Wharton, "Roman Fever"

Stories with surprise endings need not always be trivial. Faulkner's "A Rose for Emily" is a case in point, one that has been analyzed sufficiently not to require comment here, and J. D. Salinger's "A Perfect Day for Bananafish" is another.[11] And in Edith Wharton's "Roman Fever" (1934), in contrast to stories like "Marjorie Daw," the ending, instead of undermining what has preceded it, clarifies and reshapes our understanding of the entire story. In Wharton's story the ending can shape our perception of the rest of the story instead of overwhelming it.

Part of the power of Wharton's story is its apparent unobtrusiveness; it begins with a situation that implies only a mild level of conflict: "Two American ladies of ripe but well-cared-for middle age" admire the Palatine and the Forum while their two daughters, with the approval of their mothers, hurry to assignations.[12] The central problem seems to be the need of the two older women, Mrs. Slade and Mrs. Ansley, to come to terms with their age and lack of prospects for romance of their own. Their husbands are dead; they do little more than observe their daughters gad about, share memories (Mrs. Slade and Mrs. Ansley had grown up together), and get on with their knitting. A long interlude of Mrs. Slade's memories fills in background and clarifies the context of their sitting together without intensifying the forward movement of the action. After her recollections, the story returns to the present with the phrase "for a long time they continued to sit side by side without speaking" (p. 837), a line that hardly suggests conflict; it seems a marker of indirection.

But Mrs. Slade, described earlier as "the lady of high color and energetic brows," is irritated by the more placid Mrs. Ansley. One of her concerns is that Babs, Mrs. Ansley's daughter, is more "dynamic" than Mrs. Slade's own daughter Jenny. Mrs. Slade considers the Ansleys "exemplary" people (the word is used ironically—she means they are dull); she, Mrs. Slade, is the more dynamic of the older women and ought rightly to have the dynamic daughter. Then, after a discussion of Roman fever (illness, often death, caused by the supposedly malarial night air) and how Roman fever has been used in the battle for love—a great-aunt of Mrs. Ansley's reputedly sent her sister, a rival in a love affair, to gather a nightblooming flower, and thus to her death from Roman fever—Mrs. Slade breaks out: she knows why Mrs. Ansley many years ago suffered from Roman fever. Just before she married Mr. Ansley, Mrs. Ansley had kept an assignation with the (at that time) unmarried Mr. Slade. Mrs. Slade knows this, she reveals, because she herself wrote the letter that set up the assignation. She, like Mrs. Ansley's ancestor, had her own destructive hopes.

Although Mrs. Slade may think the matter can end with this revelation, it cannot; the reader, at least, needs to know Mrs. Ansley's response. But even Mrs. Slade is not finished. She is annoyed that Mrs. Ansley still seems to treasure having the letter, even though she now knows Mr. Slade did not write it. So Mrs. Slade twists the knife a bit, remarking how awful it is that Mrs. Ansley had to wait for an assignation that never took place. At this point, Mrs. Ansley gets her turn: Mr. Slade was there—she had answered his letter, and he had arranged the meeting. Mrs. Ansley has had the final word after all, and the story is sufficiently balanced that it might end. But Mrs. Slade cannot resist pointing out that Mrs. Ansley's victory is a very slim one: "I had him for twenty-five years. And you had nothing but that one letter he didn't write." To Mrs. Ansley belongs the ultimate retort: "I had Barbara" (p. 843).

The surprise ending satisfies for several reasons. It answers the question Mrs. Slade had raised on the subject of how Mrs. Ansley could have had such a lively daughter (and answers it ironically—there was outside genetic influence, as Mrs. Slade has fancifully supposed, but the dymanic genes are Mr. Slade's and Mrs. Ansley's, not hers); the placid opening is turned upside down, and all of the elements take on new significance—even Rome itself, offered only as background in the opening scene, has been part of the drama. Most significantly, the shock Mrs. Slade receives is merited. She has been driven by her own desire for superiority to ask the questions that lead to the shock; her pride has caused her downfall. The ending clarifies and binds together the beginning and the middle, revealing what in retrospect is both latent and inevitable. Indirection was only apparent; what is calm is so only as means of concealing volcanic truth. The surprise ending is successful in this story because it is responsible for making the story whole, for deepening rather than canceling what precedes it, and above all because it is thoroughly the result, and revelation, of character. Although the story may be too mechanically perfect for modern taste—it does not, as we have come to expect of short stories, work by subtlety and suggestion—nevertheless the surprise binds together theme and character, and the result is far more satisfying than the nineteenth-century examples.

Alternatives to Surprise—Indirection and Parody

Twain, "The Notorious Jumping Frog of Calaveras County"

The dependence of "Roman Fever" upon indirect form may not be accidental, for the indirect form, common in humor and in the local color movement, was primarily responsible for the health of the genre in the second half of the nineteenth century. Those who wrote surprise stories seem to have considered technical demands of the genre but were not as astutely aware of its possibilities as Twain, Sarah Orne Jewett, or Crane.

Although Twain did not describe the fiction-writing process as formally as did Poe, in "Fenimore Cooper's Literary Offenses" and in particular "How to Tell a Story," the difference he establishes between what he calls the humorous story and the comic story is the same as the distinction between the direct and indirect modes. "The humorous story," he contends, in what could serve as a definition of the indirect mode, "may be spun out to great length, and may wander around as much as it pleases, and arrive nowhere in particular"; in contrast, the comic (or what I have called "direct") story "must be brief and end with a point." Twain's own preference is for the humorous story, the mode that depends for its effect on the manner of telling. Anyone can tell a comic story, but the humorous story is a "high and delicate art."[13]

The humorous tale, a story such as "The Notorious Jumping Frog of Calaveras County" (1865), would seem to be everything that Poe disapproved of, for it not only breaks down before it reaches its end, it breaks with a vengeance. Even the first paragraph immediately sidetracks the reader, a device Twain foregrounds by having the narrator comment on it. The narrator has been asked by a friend to inquire of Simon Wheeler about a certain Leonidas W. Smiley:

> In compliance with the request of a friend of mine, who wrote me from the East, I called on good-natured, garrulous old Simon Wheeler, and inquired after my friend's friend, Leonidas W. Smiley, as requested to do, and I hereunto append the result. I have a lurking suspicion that *Leonidas W.* Smiley is a myth; that my friend never knew such a personage; and that he only conjectured that if I asked old Wheeler about him, it would remind him of his infamous *Jim* Smiley, and he would go to work and bore me to death with some exasperating reminiscence of him as long and as tedious as it should be useless to me. If that was the design, it succeeded.[14]

One of the clues to Twain's control is evident in this paragraph, for though the content is diffuse, the tonal structure is perfectly under control and is marked by an emphatic closure. Clauses pile upon one another; the level of diction momentarily lowers with the phrase "go to work and bore me to death," and the final sentence gains its effect not only by its brevity but also by the delayed arrangement and terminal impact of the final phrase, "it succeeded."

After the initial paragraph, such tonal resources are not so immediately identifiable. Although the story of *Jim* Smiley centers on Jim's betting habits, it does not seem to have its own forward direction. It is a string of incidents, first about betting on a horse, then a dog, then a frog, all organized not by the actual chronology of events in Jim's life but by Simon's immense though nearly random recall. Even the individual incidents seem indeterminate, without the subordinate closure any incident needs to be marked as complete and separate from the general flow. In Simon's account, at least, Jim never finds the stranger who loaded his frog with quail shot. Twain ends the story as Neal did "Otter-Bag"; the frame narrator simply walks away from Simon Wheeler, unwilling to submit to the beginning of yet another unshaped (read "unending") tale.

The resemblance of Twain's strategy to Neal's is only superficial. Twain has argued that the manner is what counts, and if we reexamine the tale from that perspective, we can see the story differently and detect formal tonal structure after all. Wheeler's tale of Jim, for all its apparent indirection, the way it seems to bump accidentally into its conclusion, nevertheless has a submerged sense of sequence, and that submerged quality is what Twain advocated in "How to Tell a Story": whenever the teller approaches the "nub, point, snapper, or whatever you like to call it," he must do so "in a carefully casual and indifferent way, with the pretense that he does not know it is a nub" (p. 183). An excerpt describing the extent of

Jim Smiley's desire to bet will illustrate what Twain means by "casual":

> If there was a horse-race, you'd find him flush or you'd find him busted at the end of it; if there was a dog-fight, he'd bet on it; if there was a cat-fight, he'd bet on it; if there was a chicken-fight, he'd bet on it; why, if there was two birds setting on a fence, he would bet you which one would fly first; or if there was a camp-meeting, he would be there reg'lar to bet on Parson Walker, which he judged to be the best exhorter about here, and so he was too, and a good man. If he even see a straddle-bug start to go anywheres, he would bet you how long it would take him to get to—to wherever he was going to, and if you took him up, he would foller that straddle-bug to Mexico but what he would find out where he was bound for and how long he was on the road. Lots of the boys here has seen that Smiley, and can tell you about him. Why, it never made no difference to *him*—he'd bet on *any* thing—the dangdest feller. Parson Walker's wife laid very sick once, for a good while, and it seemed as if they warn't going to save her; but one morning he come in, and Smiley up and asked him how she was, and he said she was considerable better—thank the Lord for his inf'nite mercy—and coming on so smart that with the blessing of Prov'dence she'd get well yet; and Smiley, before he thought, says, "Well, I'll resk two-and-a-half she don't anyway." [Pp. 81–82.]

The casual tone is created by the interruptions, by the continual sense of new direction. Rhetorically the speaker arranges incidents in decreasing order of significance, running from bets on subjects one traditionally bets on, horses, to less traditional ones such as chickens. The logic of the sequence is almost purely associational. What, for instance, might one think of while thinking of dogs? Cats, probably. And if cats, what next? Birds, probably, because cats eat birds. Birds do not eat chickens, but the point is to find an example slightly more improbable than the previous one, and at least chickens, vaguely associated with cockfights, are commonly bet on. Then come birds just sitting, and the issue is whether or not they will move. The next example, the reference to Parson Walker, is not part of this series, though it is needed for the terminal incident. The animal series continues with the reference to the bug and its movements, a smaller animal one more remove along the line of bettable subjects. Then Simon backs into the most unlikely situation of all, planted by the earlier reference to the parson. This situation, the possible death of the parson's wife, not a trivial subject, shocks because it is practically the most extreme case available, a case for which a bet is totally inappropriate. The pattern of this episode reveals the underlying tightness in the indirect mode, for its surprise is a combination of unexpectedness with the sudden revelation of undeniable logic. What seemed only associative is in fact the overarching concern of tonal logic, the logic of form rather than content. This method differs from that of the surprise story only in that the tangents never come to a focus, and each of the parts retains it own quality and meaning, a very significant difference.

The same controlled indirection, the same order beneath apparent disorder, is detectable in the sequence Simon has used to talk about Smiley's major betting episodes. Smiley bets on a horse, a dog, then a frog. The full force of the absurdity of betting on a frog is partly concealed for the reader (thus amplifying its impact) by Twain's use of metaphors that make the frog into other animals on which one could more plausibly bet. The frog "come down flat-footed and all right, like a cat" (p. 83), it fell to "scratching the side of his head with his hind foot," like a dog, has "fore paws," and is gifted with the fancy name Dan'l Webster. The linearity of these incidents is not in the logical sequence of actions but in the step-by-step progression of the story from reality to fantasy, from an account of the actual to fiction, from reliable testimony to an account possibly intended to gull the listener, just as the frame narrator has been gulled. The true subject of the story is storytelling itself, the teasing way a story involves us, makes us part of its world. We respond more to pattern than to sense, more to the music than the words, a vision of an endless, imaginative fecundity, bounded only by one's patience to listen. Twain's practice in "The Notorious Jumping Frog" appears to violate eight of the eighteen rules he used to judge Cooper—rules that require a tale to accomplish something and arrive somewhere, that demand all episodes be necessary, that the author will "eschew surplusage" (p. 171). These are, of course, the rules for a direct tale, in which the parts fit together clearly and obviously, and not the rules of indirection.

There were models for what Twain had done—Thomas Bangs Thorpe had strung together anecdotal kernels of tall tales into a story such as "The Big Bear of Arkansas"—but Twain made the mode his own. Thorpe, like Twain, and for that matter anyone working in the tradition of tall tales, plays on the gullibility of the listener so consistently that delay of the ending becomes a requirement of the genre. But Twain increased the density, the interrelatedness—in short, the formal aspects—of the mode. Thorpe could put together anecdotal episodes about tater hills that grow to the size of Indian mounds and corn that shoots up so fast the percussion kills a hog, all to imply what "big" means when we talk of a "big" bear, a potentially effective concatenation of episodes, but the climax—the bear dies not because he was shot but because his time has come—lacks the outrage, the ultimate irrationality, the terminal impact that characterized Twain. Twain could control forward movement in certain respects as patterned as Poe's, and all the more ingeniously and effectively for not seeming to do so at all.

Jewett, "A White Heron"

In the local color tradition, dependent as it so often was on the old-fashioned tale rather than the newer short-story pattern of Poe and Hawthorne, the indirect form is common, and nowhere is it more suitable than in Sarah Orne Jewett's "A White Heron" (1885). Even in the opening the tempo of indirection is obvious:

> The woods were already filled with shadows one June evening, just before eight o'clock, though a bright sunset still glimmered faintly among the trunks of the trees. A little girl was driving home her cow, a plodding, dilatory, provoking creature in her behavior, but a valued companion for all that. They were going away from the western light, and striking deep into the dark woods, but their feet were familiar with the path, and it was no matter whether their eyes could see it or not.[15]

The opening paragraph is tinctured with the aura of termination that characterizes the direct mode as practiced by Hawthorne: evening approaches, and a girl is on her way home. But this is not a gothic tale. Our subject is a little girl and her cow, and even if she is heading into the dark woods, the path is familiar, and she does not need to see to find it.

As the little girl goes on her way, Jewett provides a context for the scene. Every night the summer long Sylvia has had to fetch the cow home in what resembles a game of hide and seek. The story seems in no hurry to define limits, to suggest anything more than natural termination to what is only the mildest tension. In between explanations of background (Sylvia is a city-bred girl, said to be "afraid of folks" [p. 162], come for the last year to stay with her grandmother) Jewett presents Sylvia at a brook cooling her feet in the water "while the great twilight moths struck softly against her" (p. 162), a detail that implies an attack of the most harmless species of night creatures. Sylvia is in no more hurry to get home than the story is to announce its conflict.

Eventually a problem does present itself—Sylvia, "horror-stricken" (p. 163) to hear a whistle, is hailed by a young hunter who has lost his way and who wishes to spend the night at her house. The context of the interruption deepens the significance of this intrusion. Moments before she heard the whistle she was thinking of a "great red-faced boy who used to chase and frighten her" (p. 163) in the city.

The request of this young hunter, whose appearance seems the embodiment of her fears, puts her in a difficult situation. She herself is a guest in her grandmother's house, a very welcome one, but she must now present the hunter, perhaps angering her grandmother, who will discover what her granddaughter has brought home besides the cow. But once home, she finds her grandmother pleased to have a visitor, so that once again fear is put to rest rather than suspended or developed. This pattern virtually replaces the traditional need for conflict and resolution, those familiar requisites of plot. Nothing seems to establish itself as an end toward which the story may work. The reader is encouraged to assume that all potential disturbances of order are temporary, matters of perception that will soon be resolved.

At points where closure has been established—though a very weak closure, since it emerges with so little opposition or struggle—new problems are introduced. Once Sylvia is home, another potential plot emerges: the young stranger is an ornithologist, and he seeks a white heron he has seen in the neighborhood. Does Sylvia, he asks, know where it is? Jewett, with the digressiveness that has become a pattern, has Sylvia attend to a hop-toad instead of listening. The stranger repeats his request. Although she has seen the heron, she does not know where the nest is. She remains silent.

With that theme closed by Sylvia's silence, Jewett introduces another. As Sylvia and the young man go out for a walk the next day, she is charmed by him: "The woman's heart, asleep in the child, was vaguely thrilled by a dream of love" (p. 166).

This theme is introduced largely as motivation for returning to the early theme of the heron. Prompted by her new feelings, she intends to discover where the heron's nest is and to reveal it to the stranger.

The tone of the scene in which Sylvia discovers the heron's nest is charged, bristling with images, in contrast to the placid, indeterminate tone of the preceding sequences. Sylvia, who has stayed awake in order to steal out alone at night, climbs to the top of an immense pine tree, high enough to be the "great main-mast to the voyaging earth" (p. 169), and sees the ocean, woodlands, farms, church steeples, "a vast and awesome world." She is transformed into dimensions consonant with her vision; her face is "like a pale star." She is granted sight of the heron, which comes to perch himself on a bough near hers until driven away by shouting catbirds. He "goes back like an arrow presently to his home in the green world beneath" (p. 170), a good deal more directly than anything else in the story.

Just as Faulkner's Ike McCaslin gained his vision of nature from the bear, Sylvia earns hers from the heron. Her problem now takes on the recognizable shape of a conflict. On the one hand she is a woman awakened by a handsome stranger, and on the other hand she is a little girl whom a young fellow has given a penknife. Will she betray the heron for a knife? She returns home in the morning, stained with pitch from climbing the tree. The resolution Jewett provides is consonant with both the structural expectation and Sylvia's character. Sylvia says nothing. Since Sylvia's consciousness is presumably not sufficiently refined to reflect on her situation in the Jamesian manner, the narrator assists with an ironic question: "When the great world for the first time puts out a hand to her, must she thrust it aside for a bird's sake?" The quality of the resolution is in part dependent on the ironic use of the phrase "great world," for it means both the world she has glimpsed through the young hunter, the world of adulthood, the world of social contacts, the world of love, and also the world she has glimpsed from the top of the pine tree, the world of nature, of the heron.

Jewett underlines closure with a conventional device: "Many a night Sylvia heard the echo of his whistle haunting the pasture path as she came home with the loitering cow" (p. 171), a sentence that repeats the opening sequence along with the first announcement of the problem, thus encapsulating and enclosing with a time distance and a pattern of repetition. But against the triumph and inevitability of her silent choice for nature is the issue of doubt, for she is left a lonely country child. Gain in one case is balanced against loss in another.

By using the indirect mode, by allowing the end to recede and redefine itself, Jewett has found the mode appropriate to Sylvia's vision. Her world is one of repeated activities, a cow brought home night after night, a cow that might well stand as a symbol of the plot it has been put in, a plot that will not come home. Jewett comes to the point with all due deliberation. The world suggested by the heron, solemn, expansive, timeless, without "endedness," is appropriately conceived in the indirect form, with its constant sense of relocation.

Although the surprise tradition consumed the materials of fiction, wasting character and theme at the expense of effect, the ongoing tradition of indirection provided a form for experience that directness, in both pure and exaggerated surprise variations, could not include in the short story. The direct form is inherently mechanical and seems best fitted for heightened psychic experiences, not for everyday reality, for reality that is not inherently end-oriented. The indirect form has provided writers with a tradition that accommodates a broader range of experiences while still remaining subject to the laws of order and organization in reference to an endpoint.

Crane, "The Bride Comes to Yellow Sky"

The exaggerations of the surprise ending provided an easy target for the master of anticlimax, Stephen Crane, whose characters often envisage heroic action and fail miserably. Young Horace of "His New Mittens" (1898) runs away from home to escape his mother and aunt (already the choice of a child as protagonist indicates an analogy to the mode of the low burlesque, high actions mimicked by lower characters), ends up at the butcher's, is taken home, and in defeat wails for his mother. Anticlimax is not limited to the boy; the aunt, confused and embarrassed, is about to menace the butcher to hide her feelings but instead offers the butcher a root beer. Stories of this sort which invert the reader's expectation of a "snapper" at the end hardly create anything more memorable than the conventional tales they displace, but in his best fiction, Crane used parodic, anticlimactic endings to advantage, perhaps nowhere more effectively than in "The Bride Comes to Yellow Sky" (1898).[16]

The story has indirect aspects—the central problem is revealed only gradually, and some episodes are tangential—and is at the same time marked by directness. As befits the direct tradition, the pressures pointing toward a resolution are intense, all the more necessary for a story that seeks ultimately to deflate that pressure. The main characters are newlyweds on a train headed for the groom's home town, and the movement of the train "whirling onward" in the first sentence establishes a tone of urgency.[17] The actual problem to be resolved reveals itself more slowly, after a leisurely exposition of the couple's nervousness, a casual description of the furnishing of the railway car, and the amusement of the passengers and crew at what they assume to be the conventional discomfort of newlyweds. The central problem is not the honeymooners' discomfort; it is the failure of the groom, Jack Potter, marshal of Yellow Sky, to reveal to anyone in town that the purpose of his trip was to come back with a bride. As in "His New Mittens," Crane treats an essentially comic situation—what could the consequences of Potter's revelation be other than the severing of some of his former male friendships, or perhaps exposure to harmless jibes and ridicule—with the language of tragedy. The "hour of daylight," the hour to admit this "extraordinary crime" approaches; Potter prefers to put it out of mind, but the increasing familiarity of the landscape and the movement of the train make him "commensurately restless" (p. 111). When the train arrives, Potter and his wife prepare to slink into town.

Crane then shifts the point of view and the time scale, in one sense creating indirection, a tangential movement, but by the nature of the scene creating considerable forward pressure. The new focal character is a drummer in the Weary Gentleman saloon, and the scene precedes Potter's arrival by exactly twenty-one minutes. The drummer, recounting a tale of his own, is interrupted by a man who announces that Scratchy Wilson is drunk and on the loose. Through the drummer's questions the reader learns of Scratchy's desire for battle and the history of his run-ins with the marshal, all intensified by the drummer's fear for his own hide. The townsfolk engage in this retelling with such a full display of conventional be-havior—the silences, the glances, the gulp of whiskey from a bottle, the Winchester laid on top of the bar—that they may be playing on the mounting fear of the drummer. The possibility that the townsfolk may be purposely coloring the conflict to impress an outsider simply adds an edge to the tension—for in addition to the expectation of confrontation, the reader must deal with the tension of parody. A shot and three "yowls" in the distance bring the scene to a close: "There was a shuffling of feet. They looked at each other. 'Here he comes,' they said" (p. 116).

The third scene again shifts the point of view, this time to Scratchy Wilson. It has its own double-edged quality, for if Scratchy is roaring "menacing information," "cries of ferocious challenge" that ring against "walls of silence," he also wears a maroon flannel shirt "made, principally, by some Jewish women on the east side of New York" (pp. 116–17). But even if Scratchy is a man who enjoys the appearance of his rage, the comic undercutting to anyone familiar with "The Blue Hotel" does not diminish the possibility of a tragic outcome. Crane has gained much of his forward, direct motion from the anticipation of conflict; the parody increases rather than decreases that expectation. The final image of this section, Scratchy bellowing in front of Potter's empty home, "the spectacle of a man churning himself into deepest rage over the immobility of a house" (p. 118), shows the balance; the intensity of energy is in part the product of exaggeration, but that does not reduce the need for release and equilibrium.

The fourth and final scene returns to Potter and his wife, implying circularity and hence closure. Potter, slinking up to the house in hope of sliding in unobserved, is met with a revolver on his chest. Potter, Scratchy claims menacingly, has been sneaking up on him, and Scratchy will not accept Potter's excuses. Why has Potter no gun? "Married," Potter says. The way Crane closes by controlling the rhythms of this final scene is best observed in a substantial portion:

> "Married?" said Scratchy. Seemingly for the first time he saw the drooping drowning woman at the other man's side. "No!" he said. He was like a creature allowed a glimpse of another world. He moved a pace backward, and his arm with the revolver dropped to his side. "Is this—is this the lady?" he asked.
>
> "Yes, this is the lady," answered Potter.
>
> There was another period of silence.
>
> "Well," said Wilson at last, slowly, "I s'pose it's all off now."
>
> "It's all off if you say so, Scratchy. You know I didn't make the trouble." Potter lifted his valise.
>
> "Well, I 'low it's off, Jack," said Wilson. He was looking at the ground. "Married!" He was not a student of chivalry; it was merely that in the presence of this foreign condition he was a

simple child of the earlier plains. He picked up his starboard revolver, and placing both weapons in their holsters, he went away. His feet made funnel-shaped tracks in the heavy sand. [P. 120.]

Crane winds down the tension by repetitions and silences and provides commentary and evaluation in contrast to the banality of the dialogue. The out-of-place reference to "starboard" revolver suggests through the shifted frame of reference to sea gear something of the decorativeness of the scene, and the image of the "funnel-shaped tracks" creates terminal significance, suggesting a comic, even childlike determination on the part of Scratchy, as well as providing a firm contrast, in its slow recession, to the whirling image of the Pullman of the opening paragraph.

The anticlimax of the ending has been carefully prepared for. That gunplay was a public ritual, not always played with deadly intent, was implicit in the scene in the Weary Gentleman saloon. What triumphs here is common sense; the world of domesticity, of marriage, cancels the games male grownups like to play with guns. The conventions of the western shootout, which are a classic example of direct, end-oriented pressure, have been turned to make a much quieter point. It is a valise, not a pistol, that Potter raises.

The ending implies something about the relation of endings in fiction to endings in life that James would later make more explicit. The characters in Crane's novels as well as his stories often swell with delusions, some of them never adjusting to an accurate sense of the realities of war or the struggle with nature.[18] One way to express this vision is to invert linear narrative tale, for part of Crane's point is that a mistaken linearity derived from a fictional convention, which expresses our hopes without reference to our conditions, is what sustains our delusions. Life brings down our expectations, and the appropriate vehicle for the discovery of our limitations is the anticlimactic ending.

CHAPTER 4

Converging Closure and the Theory of Openness

James, "Paste," "A Bundle of Letters," "Four Meetings," "The Altar of the Dead"

Like Crane, James disdained the terminal surprises of Aldrich, Bunner, or O. Henry. Although he had written surprise stories—"Master Eustace" (1871) reveals that the stepfather of Master Eustace, a young man with a spoiled child's possessiveness of his mother, is in fact his real father—James later chose not to emphasize the revelation of circumstance. When he did work with material that lent itself to surprise—in "Paste" (1899), for instance, a story James modeled partly after Maupassant's "The Necklace," a prime example of the surprise ending—James defused the impact of termination.[1] Mme Loisel of Maupassant's story discovers at the end that the jewels she has borrowed, lost, and replaced at the cost of ten years of labor were merely paste; James, in "Paste," immediately raises the issue of the genuineness of the jewels, as the title implies, focusing the story on the meaning of the jewels to each of the characters. If they are real, then Arthur Prime's stepmother, who had once been on the stage, probably was less than virtuous before her marriage to Arthur's clergyman father. Arthur's cousin Charlotte, to whom he has given the jewels, is the character on whom pressure to determine their genuineness is applied, primarily by Mrs. Guy, a friend of Charlotte's. Charlotte would be more pleased if the one pearl necklace that has caught everyone's attention were paste so that she would not have to confront Arthur with an unsettling view of his mother. After she gives the pearls back to him, Arthur later tells her he has had them examined, has learned they were paste, and has had them smashed. But the necklace ultimately appears on Mrs. Guy's neck, and not, Charlotte believes, because Mrs. Guy bought them, as she maintains, on Bond Street. Arthur, Charlotte suspects, has dealt with Mrs. Guy directly. Charlotte, so concerned over the niceties of her own conduct, discovers no one else has such scruples.

Maupassant counts only on the impact of the emotion that must dominate Mme Loisel at the moment of revelation, the despair over the erasure of all her effort. At the end of "Paste" Charlotte may well suffer her own despair, but James has entitled Charlotte to more varied and positive emotions, providing a sense of the moral consistency of Charlotte, who should well survive her revelation. James has focused on character, Maupassant on the single emotion of a character. Maupassant, in the tradition of the surprise story, has brought everything to focus on a single moment; James has depended on accumulation.

After his initial apprenticeship, whenever James had the opportunity to create surprise endings in stories, he declined it. The revelation in "The Altar of the Dead" (1895) that the one person George Stransom refuses to light a candle for is the very one his unnamed female co-worshiper wishes to honor could well have ended an O. Henry story, but James put the discovery in the middle and concentrated on working out the moral consequences of this coincidence. To emphasize the ending at the expense of the rest of the story would have been inconsistent with principles he expressed in "The Art of Fiction," in which he characterized the medium as "a living thing, all one and continuous, like any other organism, and in proportion as it lives will it be found, I think, that in each of the parts there is something of each of the other parts."[2] By parts James meant description, dialogue, and incident, and it was the need for the proper interaction of these elements that led him to argue that a story could not be composed as a "series of blocks." Stretching James's word "parts" to include beginnings, middles, and ends does not distort his original meaning. Endings are one feature of a story he explicitly discusses in the essay, expressing his contempt for happy endings, the distribution of prizes, as if endings were nothing more than "a course of dessert and ices."[3] The menu analogy, with its slots for interchangeable, predictable elements, represents exactly what James has rejected; his own analogies for literary structure, more organic ones, stress wholeness, interrelatedness, and uniqueness.

James fashioned his stories with the end in mind much as Poe had, as an examination of the working methods described in his notebooks reveals. The germ of a Jamesian story was often an anecdote or an idea, and generally James projected an action that would develop the idea into a story, culminating in a denouement, sometimes projected as a pious hope, as illustrated in the entry on the anecdote that sparked the story "Brooksmith" (1891): "Represent this—the refined nature of the plain quiet woman—her appreciation—and the way her new conditions sicken her, with denouement if possible."[4] More commonly he specifically supplied the ending in his notebook while he began to alter and shape the original anecdotes. In "The Real Thing" (1892)—a story stemming from an anecdote about an aristocratic couple who, having fallen on hard times, seek to earn money by offering themselves to painters as models for aristocratic characters—James, after trying to focus on the couple, then preferred to concentrate on the need of the painter to gain a particularly important commission. This decision in turn enabled James to arrive at a suitable denouement, the painter's announcement that "the

melancholy Major and his wife won't do—they're not 'in it' ";
the aristocrats are less suitable than a pair of commoners with a
flair for imitation.[5]

But rejection of the surprise ending did not lead James to
experiment with endings in the structure of the short story, a
remarkable fact given what he had done with endings in the
novel. James's efforts in that genre have been carefully chron-
icled. One critic, Marianna Torgovnick, has studied the
closural techniques James used in his novels, detailing "the
gradual process of artistic self-discovery that allowed James to
realize fully his own characteristic form of ending—the scenic
ending, bare of authorial commentary, focused intently on the
final conversation of two protagonists, and rich in formal connections to the body of the novel—a process that included
playing with and working through the popular nineteenth-
century forms of ending he despised."[6] She persuasively argues that after his initial and relatively conventional efforts in
the short story and novel, James rejected the traditional Vic-
torian epilogue in favor of the scenic presentation without
authorial mediation, a method that forces the reader to review
the story retrospectively and thus finally assemble for himself
the story's end. In *The Portrait of a Lady,* for example, the reader
must resolve for himself what Caspar Goodwood is thinking
and will do after he hears Henrietta Stackpole's "just you
wait."[7]

Because her topic is the novel, Torgovnick mentions the
endings of James's short stories only in passing. In fact, James
uses conventional means to end his short stories, and this in
itself reveals much about James's view of the short story and
provides an interesting puzzle. James proposed theories about
fiction, life, and open-endedness, but his practice in the short
story in this regard was similar to Poe's. Critics have maintained for some time that James was no innovator in short
fiction—Arthur Voss, for example, contends that James did
not contribute "as much to modifying radically the short-

story form as writers like Chekhov, Joyce, and Katherine Mansfield"—but why his theory and practice were so different is a subject worth investigating.[8]

In principle, James's techniques ought to be the same for both short and long fiction. James argues, as did Poe, that singleness of effect is essential for a short story—in the notebooks he pleads with himself when contemplating a short story to take "only the single incident . . . to make use, for the brief treatment, of nothing, absolutely *nothing,* that isn't ONE, as it were—that doesn't begin and end in its little self."[9] But unlike Poe or Brander Matthews, James did not regard the short story as distinctly different from longer forms. The distinctions between short and longer forms he believed were merely quantitative, not qualitative.[10] The New York Edition simply discriminates between novels and tales; James makes no distinction between a very short tale and his favorite form, the nouvelle, which he defined as only an idea with a length proper to itself.[11] In "The Art of Fiction" James had argued that the various aspects of fiction—character and plot, for instance—were inseparably related; he seemed to believe that the various genres of fiction also operated under very much the same laws regardless of length.

Although he did not regard the genre as qualitatively distinct from longer forms, he did distinguish between several forms of short fiction, one of which he clearly preferred over the other. As he put the matter in an introduction to a collection of stories by Hubert Crackanthorpe:

> The short tale . . . may be, like the long one, mainly of two sorts: the chain of items, figures in a kind of sum . . . added up as on a school-boy's slate and with the correct total and its little flourish constituting the finish and accounting for the effect; or else it may be an effort preferably pictorial, a portrait of conditions, an attempt to summarize and compress for purposes of presentation, to "render" even, if possible, for purposes of expression.[12]

In his later review of a collection of stories by Henry Harland, he again posited two types of short stories:

> The one with which we are most familiar is that of the detached incident, single and sharp, as clear as a pistol-shot; the other, of rarer performance, is that of the impression, comparatively generalized—simplified, foreshortened, reduced to a particular perspective—of a complexity or a continuity. The former is an adventure comparatively safe, in which you have, for the most part, but to put one foot after the other. It is just the risks of the latter, on the contrary that make the best of the sport. These are naturally—given the general reduced scale— immense, for nothing is less intelligible than bad foreshortening, which if it fails to mean everything intended, means less than nothing.[13]

In both cases the form he prefers, termed "pictorial" in the Crackanthorpe essay and "foreshortened" in the Harland review, seems the same, that is, a form short and simple on the surface but one which cleverly condenses complex experiences. The forms he denigrates in each essay may not be identical—the Crackanthorpe essay seems to refer to the conventional tale pattern, which arranges a series of events in chronological form, perhaps tightened as it was by contemporary practitioners and perhaps marked by a surprise (the "flourish"?) at the end. The Harland review seems to refer to something slightly different—to short stories that achieve their restrictions by mirroring events themselves restricted, "detached." Neither of these alternatives interested James; he admired only the foreshortened form, which he thought would allow him to condense the substance of a longer tale into a brief one. He wanted to shape the work with his own form, not merely to write about incidents that were small and slight in themselves. The foreshortened form is not distinguished from similar novelistic techniques—the short story is simply a more highly compressed version.

James's theories about endings for all lengths of fiction, elaborated in the notebooks and prefaces, were striking in their novelty. James argued, as had none of his predecessors, that endings revealed the artificiality of fiction. "The *whole* of everything is never told; you can only take what groups together," he claimed in his notebook.[14] Fiction may have endings, but life does not. He put the point even more forcefully in his preface to *Roderick Hudson:* "Really, universally, relations stop nowhere, and the exquisite problem of the artist is eternally to draw, by a geometry of his own, the circle within which they shall happily *appear* to do so."[15] The logical extension of this view is that closure can be achieved satisfactorily without recourse to resounding finality, without having all aspects of the story converge at the end, neatly rounded off with the death of the protagonist. The beginning, middle, and end might conceivably be detached from the flow of events recounted in the story; form could be separated from content. This view seems in line with the twentieth-century short story, particularly as written by Anderson, Faulkner, and Katherine Anne Porter, for whom the circle drawn by the story does not circumscribe the implied events. A story could then be open, that is, perceived as complete, while still suggesting continuity.

James did write stories that illustrate this principle of the author's special geometry—"A Bundle of Letters" (1879) is a case in point. Life in Mme de Maisonrouge's pension is clearly a "bundle" that receives its packaged identity largely from James's arrangement. There are six major characters, three young women (two American, one British) and three young men (American, French, and German), and each in a letter to a friend characterizes several of the other pensioners. Only one emerges as more significant than the rest, the American girl, Miranda Hope, and that only because James grants her more letters than the others and grants them the honored positions of first and last, a very simple piece of geometry. The only action completed in the story is the announcement at the end that Miranda has received a letter from a young man whose failure to write was one of her complaints in the opening of the story. Repeated phrases also suggest pure circularity without progress. "Dear mother, my money holds out very well, and it *is* real interesting," she writes to end her first letter.[16] She concludes the last with, "Dearest mother, my money holds out, and it *is* most interesting" (p. 533). The minor verbal differences enforce identity, not difference. The story also seems complete because of the broad range of views of each character, a device that suggests completion by antithesis. According to one character, "Mme. Maisonrouge belongs to one of the oldest and proudest families in France, but has had reverses which have compelled her to open an establishment" (p. 499), while according to another, she is "high-shouldered and short-necked and literally hideous," was probably "a paid book-keeper," and "in spite of her smiles and the pretty things she says to every one, she hates us all and would like to murder us" (p. 509). Views of the relative value of various national experiences are similarly opposed. Bostonian Louis Leverett finds virtue only in European forms, in European landscapes, and in the English girls' clothes, while New Englander Miranda Hope intends to concentrate on Europe only momentarily. She is keeping Boston to "finish off" herself and hopes to talk to Leverett to get a "peep now and then in advance" (p. 606) of the real Boston, a conversation we cannot imagine Leverett relishing.

James's geometry here easily takes the measure of a static subject. This sense of completeness and closure, however, describes only the formal aspects of the piece. The actual telling of the story ends nothing for the characters, whose lives are seen as continuing in flux. A whole has been created by a series of juxtaposed viewpoints, wholeness suggested by the balance of the telling.

But "A Bundle of Letters" is not typical of James, and the

thinness of the story may offer one reason why he did not continue to write short fiction in this vein. The method did not suggest the depth which changes over time could more easily create. More commonly James relied on conventional geometry. "Four Meetings" (1877), for instance, the story of Caroline Spencer, the New England spinster whose desire to visit Europe is never fulfilled, has its limits immediately established by the reference to Caroline's death. The difference between this story and "A Bundle of Letters" is that "Four Meetings" moves in clearly linear time—eighteen years—and the ending is an ironic reversal, an inversion of the opening. In the beginning Caroline Spencer wishes to see Europe; in the end, Europe has descended on her, in the form of the "countess" Caroline's cousin had married, a cruel imposition on her charity. Here the geometry of form is congruent with a life pattern of the character, and all the essentials of the pattern are observable, including the natural termination, death.

The structure of "Four Meetings" is far more typical of James than is "A Bundle of Letters." Poe's standard for the short story—his emphasis on natural termination, linear progress, and convergence—became more, not less, James's own standard through the latter part of the century. Morgan Moreen in "The Pupil" (1891), his little heart exhausted either, as his parents claim, from the long walk he took with his tutor Pemberton or from the shock of seeing his wandering parents thrown out of their hotel and himself indefinitely loaned to Pemberton, expires on the last page. Dencombe, the novelist of "The Middle Years" (1893), no sooner comes to his revelation: "We do what we can—we give what we have" (9:75–76), his words "barely audible," then he too expires. Stransom from "The Altar of the Dead" (1895) rises from his sickbed for one final meeting with his co-worshiper, then collapses in her arms, his face marked with "the whiteness of death." John Marcher of "The Beast in the Jungle" (1903) throws himself on

May Bartram's grave as he senses the approach of the Beast: "His eyes darkened—it was close; and, instinctively turning, in his hallucination to avoid it, he flung himself, on his face, on the tomb" (11:402). Marcher's death is not literal, but it is certainly a death wish. To argue that relations in these stories stop nowhere would be difficult—James wrings the life from his protagonists at the end of their struggles, following the curve of their lives to the grave. The structure of the telling parallels the structure of the characters' life spans, thus allowing James the depth and completeness he desired within his enclosed tale, so that he could expend, as Poe had, as much effort on making every aspect of the story work toward termination.

In "The Altar of the Dead," for instance, the metaphor of the altar forms one of the linear strands that has its own independent form of development and climax. At first, the altar that Stransom conceives to honor his dead is purely metaphoric, raised in his "spiritual spaces" (9:233). James develops the metaphor so elaborately that the altar begins to seem real, and then the altar does take an actual form—Stransom finds a church and persuades the ecclesiastics to have a chapel maintained at his expense. The candles on the altar continue to grow in their intensity (grow, that is, largely in Stransom's perception) so that they "flare" and "dazzle" and "blind" (p. 269) and finally "speak in a passion of light—they sing out like a choir of angels" (p. 271). Tonally the image that concludes "The Altar of the Dead" resembles "The Fall of the House of Usher." The all-consuming blaze of candles at the end is more inward and mental than the crashing end of the House of Usher, as befits the inward psychological turn James gave to fiction, but both Usher and Stransom have brought down their worlds with an obsession with death, and both end their lives in the grasp of their sisterly women. In James, the gothicism is absent—the woman of "The Altar of the Dead" is without blood on her lips and has not lately returned from the dead—and Stransom's death suggests purgation and salvation.

The ideas James had expressed about the short story in the Harland and Crackanthorpe excerpts seem to explain his rejection of open endings in the short story. In these essays James could not accept the idea of a short story as a single incident; he preferred to emphasize the pictorial, the foreshortened representation of a large and complex action. Once committed to a linear approach, and one that characteristically covered a large portion of a character's life, he was committed to roundedness, to a compressed but fully representative form. An image from "The Altar of the Dead" expresses the dilemma. Stransom's co-worshiper would settle for a single candle on her altar; Stransom needs a full complement, and he needs to experiment and readjust the candles until he achieves a perfect symmetry, a form without "the disfigurement of a possible gap" (p. 268). James's desire to shape a story is closely parallel to Stransom's desire to find the perfectly balanced display of his candles. Like Stransom, he rejects the single candle that characterizes "the single sharp shot" method. James's desire to fill in the gaps, to commit himself to foreshortened form that will despite its brevity suggest fullness, led him to an intensity of repetition far removed from the open scenic ending.

Paradoxically, once James posited an identity between the novel and the short story, he demanded more of himself in the short story than in the novel. His concern to avoid "bad foreshortening" might have been so much on his mind in writing the short story that the problem was more a matter of how much he could get in than what he could leave out. It is no wonder he would liken the effort of staying under six thousand words in a tale to "the anxious effort of some warden of the insane engaged at a critical moment in making fast a victim's straitjacket."[17] Given the need to compress a complete and significant experience into a small form, he could not, as

Chekhov had, simply lop off the conventional ending. Fiction required the exploration of character, and "character is interesting as it comes out, and by the process and duration of that emergence"; such a character study requires moral development, "dreadful as such a prospect might loom for a poor interpreter committed to brevity."[18] As H. G. Ruthrof has argued, James feared that "brevity is achieved at the expense of some other literary value."[19] His skill as a short-story writer, and it is immense, allowed him only to elaborate old forms, not to initiate new ones. Open endings such as he had used in his novels could be designed for the short story only by others who conceived of the short story as distinct from the novel.

Convergence: Retrospection and New Directions

In the endings used by Poe and Hawthorne, natural termination and convergence of closural signals on the endpoint dominate, and so it is easy to see why James, and others as well, would fall back upon these devices even though their theories or capabilities might have otherwise led them elsewhere. The pattern is so dominant that even those stories that do not end with the death of the protagonist, those that presumably imply continuation, are rarely as open as they might seem.

In many of Poe's stories, fictions are designed to self-destruct so that there will be no question of what follows. Not only is Roderick Usher dragged down by his sister Madeline, but the whole house collapses, disappearing from sight. Although the number of such extreme cases in Poe is not large—in "The Masque of the Red Death" (1842) Prince Prospero falls prostrate, revelers drop in "blood-bedewed halls" (p. 676), the clock stops ticking, the flames of the tripods expire, and "Darkness and Decay and the Red Death held illimitable dominion over all" (p. 677)—there are a significant number. "The Oval Portrait" (1842) ends with the painter exclaiming that he has created a picture of life itself, while failing to note that his sitter (his wife) has just died. In "William Wilson" (1839), the title character stabs his double but finds himself exclaiming that he has just murdered himself. "The Cask of Amontillado" (1846) ends with Fortunato walled up in Montressor's vault, the last stone forced into position, a rampart of bones heaped before the vault.

Poe's stories that do not end in annihilation sometimes seem defective: one of the shortcomings of "The Pit and the Pendulum" (1843) is the sudden rescue by General Lasalle. Although we can accept this conclusion because we would like to see the narrator saved, clearly the logic of the end was closing in on him in the very literal form of the walls. Even though the narrator survives, the ending does not imply anything more than a superficial continuity. The narrator, like many Poe protagonists, is not endowed with living traits and ordinary acts or concerns, so that when we leave the obsession on which the story focuses, even if the character survives, he remains as nothing more than the teller of a tale. Even in a story with an apparent openness, little actually exists. In "Ligeia" (1838), which achieves its antithetical fullness not by the usual reversal of life into death but by the reversal of death, the return of Ligeia to life, the action of the story is not complete but just beginning. But one cannot imagine anything resembling conventional housekeeping for the reunited couple. (They were hardly conventional before her return, but even reading and lounging about after she returns seem difficult to imagine under the circumstances.) The only recourse for the narrator would be to blot out the experience, to go mad, which he seems to be on the verge of doing as he shrieks her name.[20] The openness is only an illusion. Poe is not saying "imagine this couple afterward"; he achieves his effect by demonstrating how inconceivable continuity would be.

Hawthorne, too, frequently sends his characters to the

grave, leaving Father Hooper a veiled corpse in his coffin, pushing the last breath out of Georgiana as the crimson tint of her birthmark fades, and not only having Ethan Brand leap into the limekiln, where the next morning his skeleton is found, but also permitting the lime-burner to poke about with his stick and crumble the relics into fragments. Hawthorne varied his removal of the final traces of his characters more than did Poe—sometimes lamely, as in "Celestial Rail-road," in which the narrator discovers the entire story was a dream, or more imaginatively by making the death metaphoric, with the townsfolk carrying off Major Molineux, tarred and feathered. Molineux survives, though the revelry in his passing is linked to "mockery round some dead potentate" (11:230). Young Goodman Brown (1835) emerges from his nocturnal ordeal technically alive, but he might as well have been dead, for he has become a stern, desperate man, turning away from family and friends, spending the rest of his life in gloom. Characters may survive, as does the couple at the end of "The May-Pole of Merry Mount" (1836), but both Robin and the couple face the future with their past, which has been the subject of the story, obliterated.

There are exceptions to this pattern in Hawthorne, and they are worth considering. "Rappaccini's Daughter" (1844), for instance, could well have ended with Beatrice giving up her last breath after the fashion of the other wronged angels of Hawthorne's fiction, but Hawthorne brings in Baglioni, the scientist who had given Giovanni the antidote that killed Beatrice. The reader here is given the task of completing the significance of the Baglioni's question—"'Rappaccini! Rappaccini! and is *this* the upshot of your experiment!'"—a task that normally is done by Hawthorne himself in the morals drawn in the final paragraph. It is for the reader to realize that Baglioni is as much to blame for the death as Rappaccini, that those who are "good" have as much poison in them, as Beatrice pointed out to Giovanni, as those who are evil. This, however, is suspended judgment, not suspended action.

In "Wakefield" (1835) Hawthorne suspends the action. Wakefield returns to the bosom of his family after an absence of twenty years, a return more spontaneous than premeditated, for Wakefield, chilled and wet, returns more to warm himself than for any other reason. The narrator withdraws from the action—"We will not follow our friend across the threshold" (9:140)—teasing us into wondering what the future will hold for Wakefield. But the continuity is largely imaginary, for the narrator has thrown the weight of his moralizing against Wakefield, cautioning the reader to realize that although Wakefield might "deem himself the same man as ever" (p. 135), he deludes himself. Ironically, despite his return, Wakefield will remain "Outcast of the Universe" (p. 140). Hawthorne creates the illusion of an open ending but in effect predicts that the outcome will be the same as Young Goodman Brown's—a death in life. "My Kinsman, Major Molineux" is a significant exception to this pattern, and I comment on the story in more detail later at the end of a discussion of Porter's "Flowering Judas."

James varied the pattern of complete convergence and annihilation even more than Hawthorne, but he was still dominated by it. Sometimes he began stories with the death of the central subject established; "The Four Meetings" (1877), "Brooksmith" (1891), and "Greville Fane" (1892) are typical examples. Sometimes, as in Hawthorne, the death is metaphorical; the absence of the Monarchs, who clearly might as well be dead, for their aristocracy does not make them fit representatives for the artistic portrayal of it—closes off "The Real Thing" (1892). Sometimes the death is that of a part of oneself, as in "The Jolly Corner" (1908). When ending a story with an actual death, James customarily stops the story just short of the full discovery of death. "Poor Dencombe was barely audible" in "The Middle Years" (1893), but his words

mark "the virtual end of his first and only chance" at writing
the books he has wanted to. Stransom in "The Altar of the
Dead" (1895) whispers his final words, but it is left to his
accomplice to realize what has happened: "A great dread was
on her of what might still happen, for his face had the whiteness of death" (9:271).

Stories from the nineteenth century that leave open the possibility of further action are primarily those in the indirect
form, that is, those that postpone endings, those whose shape
is primarily derived from the more leisurely tale pattern. We
do not learn the actual ending to the Jim Smiley story in "The
Notorious Jumping Frog"; instead, Jim sets out after the man
who tricked him. The sense of continuity is further increased
because it is a frame story and the narrator walks away from
another story that is just beginning. In Jewett's "White
Heron," the action of the story is completed, the hunter has
left, but the feeling of continuity dominates. The central action was a negation, not a completion; Sylvia declined to show
the nest of the heron to the hunter. The narrator approaches
the end with an encapsulation that underlines continuity and
uncertainty—"Many a night Sylvia heard the echo of his whistle haunting the pasture path." The narrator concludes not
with a statement but a question—"Were the birds better
friends than their hunter might have been,—who can tell?"
(p. 171). Indirectness, however, with its more open ending and
leisurely progress, is a relatively minor pattern. The convergence of closure and the steady progress toward the ending
are the dominant features of major nineteenth-century short
stories.

Inevitably, though, firm closural patterns and convergence
gave way to alternatives. James had seen that the firm closural
pattern of traditional narrative could rarely be applied to the
world of human actions outside of fiction. For him the issue
was not that narrative falsified our view of the world but that
causal chains were far more complex and subtle than direct

linear patterns of fiction. In response to this disparity between world and art, James in his novels "subtlized" art, constructed fictions that more nearly represented the action of the mind, its restricted view, its hesitations, doubts, and constant need to probe and reconstruct in order to understand. This recognition led to a renewal of narrative form, though for reasons cited in the last chapter, not an alteration of the short-story form.

From our perspective in the late twentieth century, it is easy to see how much the form of the short story has changed. A thoroughly justifiable explanation of changes particularly noticeable by the 1920s can be constructed solely on the basis of the normal tendency of artists to seek maximum impact and expressiveness. In the words of one critic who has studied the changes in short-story form, Austin Wright, "The explanation most pertinent to a study of artistic developments is simply that the writers of the twenties were trying to produce more compelling and more memorable works of art."[21] Wright, whose study encompasses hundreds of stories, all analyzed for changes in techniques such as flashbacks or relative changes in the balance of scene and summary, argues that the compression of the short story of the twentieth century was a slow and logical growth:

> By using the small action, the illuminating episode, as a unifying principle, the writers of the twenties reduced the amount of activity or incident necessary to bring their stories to completion. Thus they had more scope for the development of character and thought—they were freer to choose for their stories situations involving such elements. It was an attempt to sharpen and concentrate the focus of the short story—to find the unifying principle most appropriate to the absolute magnitude of the short story, most capable of yielding that sort of concentrated richness that we are accustomed to find in great art. In the course of this attempt they brought the short story much closer to the nature of the lyric poem.[22]

Accurate as Wright's analysis might be, other explanations are possible. Changes in attitudes toward closure, I believe, have also had much to do with alterations in the form of the short story. In part our feelings about closure have changed for external reasons, because we think differently about causality and finality. The Jamesian vision of the world outside of fiction still presumes that human affairs can be understood by applying a cause-and-effect analysis, a view that has not always been shared in the twentieth century. More and more often writers wrote about characters from whose vantage point causality did not seem to apply. In Sherwood Anderson's "Sophistication," for instance, George Willard sees "countless figures of men who before his time have come out of nothingness into the world, lived their lives and again disappeared into nothingness." George knows that "in spite of all the stout talk of his fellows he must live and die in uncertainty, a thing blown by the winds, a thing destined like corn to wilt in the sun."[23] This is a vision of the end of things, but a personal apocalypse without redemption. George sees beginnings and endings but has no sense of middles or of any relation of beginning to ending. His view is confirmed as he looks around himself, standing at the fairground with Helen White: "The place has been filled to overflowing with life. It has itched and squirmed with life and now it is night and the life has all gone away. The silence is almost terrifying" (p. 240).

Narrative clearly rests on the idea of causality, on a series of steps toward a recognizable end. As views similar to those of Gertrude Stein, who wanted writers to concentrate on evoking a sense of presence, a sense of the power of the moment independent of its context, gained currency, narrative form was bound to change.[24] Endings would inevitably become more open, and if, as I have argued, the ending is the primary determinant of the shape of the structure as a whole, then the structure as a whole would also change.

If writers' awareness of endings was instrumental in the

creation of the nineteenth-century short story, a negative awareness is the key to the connection between endings and structure and to the new forms that characterize modern short fiction. The problem for the writer—and this problem will be the theme of the second half of this study—was not to count on the reader's awareness of progression toward climax and to close the story with finality and completeness, leaving no residue other than what was required to force the reader back into the story to understand the thematic content; the problem was to disguise movement toward the end and to disguise closure so as to imply that relations have no end. Wright's explanation of change adequately explains the compactness of many twentieth-century stories, but it does not account for the structural variety of the new forms as well as changing attitudes toward closure does.

Significantly, though, the changes in narrative form do not always turn out to be extensive. Even in dealing with radically altered endings—from "Flowering Judas," dominated by the gluttonous bulk of the seated Braggioni, to the ambiguous ending of Malamud's "Magic Barrel," with Leo Finkle rushing, flowers in hand, to Stella Salzman, to Nancy sitting in her rocking chair in Faulkner's "That Evening Sun," and to the chamber of commerce catalogs in William Gass's "In the Heart of the Heart of the Country"—familiar narrative patterns reappear. Arthur Kinney has argued that Faulkner used "traditional linear arrangements of fiction as an understood subtext toward which the reader is always driving his impressions and judgments," and this view can be extended in varying degrees to many other authors.[25] If nothing else, familiar narrative expectations, as they are progressively frustrated, serve to indicate the extent of a departure from a norm.

This interplay of the text and the reader's narrative expectations will engage us in the reader's response even more than in the first half of this book. The reader must often apply the five methods—solution of the problem, natural termination, antithesis, manifestation of a moral or theme, and encapsulation—in new ways. The reader, too, must often deal with the open story, the story that seems to extend beyond the end-point. Limits obtain here as well, and I have chosen stories that push the reader to these limits—twentieth-century writers have thrived on challenging the reader. My examples in this half of this study in no sense catalog all the possibilities, but they should suggest the variety of closural techniques and structures available to modern writers.

CHAPTER 5

The Twentieth Century:
New Forms

Imagist Form

Anderson, "Hands"

"We had pretty much chucked the old gods and wanted new ones," Sherwood Anderson claimed. The old ways of writing would not suffice: "The plot notion did seem to me to poison all story telling. What I wanted I thought was form, not plot."[1] Plot, by implication, wrapped things up too neatly. What he needed, to use academic terms in place of Anderson's breezier diction, was a more flexible approach to closure. He needed to be able to end a story without producing a structure that consumed itself. He needed, in James's words, the geometry that would still allow him to suggest continuity.

Creating form without plot was a continual struggle for him, but at times he succeeded. One of his methods was to break narrative into flashbacks dominated by a central image or tableau, as in "Hands" (1916), the initial story of *Winesburg, Ohio*. Looked at from the point of view of its own time, "Hands," the story of the restless hands of Wing Biddlebaum, is unique in that so little seems to happen to Wing, whose anxiety, like that of most of the other inhabitants of Winesburg, is finally unresolved.

To create this suspension, Anderson did not abruptly over-throw tradition; like any revolutionary he reassembled older forms into new patterns, clearly shaping parts of "Hands" in conventional narrative form. The section that explains the real name of Wing Biddlebaum (Adolph Myers) and how Wing came to fear his hands is a summary with conventional chronological organization that ends with Wing driven from his home town in Pennsylvania by people "swearing and throwing sticks and great balls of soft mud at the figure that screamed and ran faster and faster in the darkness."[2] They have concluded that his need to touch the boys in his school is a perversion, and they have expelled him. In another section, Wing realizes that his hands rest on George's shoulders, and he leaves George, declaring, "I can talk no more with you" (p. 30), a section similarly conventional and complete in itself. Both scenes underline termination by flight; Wing exits, as if from a stage scene.

But Anderson does not tell the story by arranging these complete sections in chronological order. Instead, he creates a frame, the image of Wing walking back and forth on his veranda. The narrator speaks repeatedly of the "story of Wing Biddlebaum," a story that is "worth a book in itself," a story that "needs the poet" (p. 29) to tell—a story, in short, that ought to be told, but not the one the humble narrator, no poet or storyteller himself, could tell, a device that allows Anderson to order his story without reference to chronological progression.

The use of an image as a frame greatly restricts the extent of the action that occurs in the "real" time of the story (real as opposed to the time of flashback incidents). Wing leaves the veranda momentarily—he crosses a field and looks along a road in hope of seeing George Willard—but he returns immediately to his porch by the second paragraph of the story. At the end of the story he goes inside to eat, returning afterward to the porch.

This embedding technique alters the forward pressure of the narrative. Most obviously, the pressure is reduced. Even the opening image, that of "a fat little old man" walking "nervously up and down" (p. 27) implies movement in itself, not movement toward an end. Like any opening sentence of a short story constructed with the singleness advocated by Poe, the first sentence predicts actions and themes, though it foreshadows not specific actions but circularity and irresolution, exactly what the story delivers. In the same way, forward direction is not abandoned but transformed, forcing the reader to wonder not about "what next" but about "why." Why does Wing walk back and forth? Why is Wing so narrowly identified with hands "forever active, forever striving to conceal themselves" (p. 28), their action as pointless as his walking? Each of the two blocks of conventional narrative illustrates the motion of the hands and terminates with an incomplete act, first, Wing enigmatically leaving George and then the Pennsylvania incident, which repeats and clarifies the hand problem. The pressure for resolution is further intensified by the presence of a narrator striving to organize his thoughts, hoping that the talk of hands "will arouse the poet who will tell the hidden wonder story" they represent (p. 31). The narrator, as he gropes for meaning, alerts the reader to the need to reconstruct meaning for himself.

To terminate the movement inherent in the veranda image of Wing is in one sense a problem and in another sense not. It is not problematic insofar as the story is read as a Freudian document. As in psychoanalytic therapy, a habitual gesture, a neurosis, has been uncovered and a past incident identified as at least partially the source. The discovery is the equivalent of drawing a moral, deriving an abstract lesson, and as such is an analogue for completion. On the other hand, the story is incomplete, and the cure incomplete, in that the gesture remains, the patient still suffers. Wing remains on the porch, walking, moving. The circumstances of that walking and the way movements are described suggest termination, or more precisely a sense of frozen motion, of the termination of our need to watch further, even though the action itself is ongoing and unresolved. Anderson depends on circularity (a form of antithesis), returning Wing to the porch after the insert scenes, and uses a sunset (natural termination) along with that return. In the final sentences, Anderson encapsulates the scene by metaphor:

> A few stray white bread crumbs lay on the cleanly washed floor by the table; putting the lamp upon a low stool he began to pick up the crumbs, carrying them to his mouth one by one with unbelievable rapidity. In the dense blotch of light beneath the table, the kneeling figure looked like a priest engaged in some service of his church. The nervous expressive fingers, flashing in and out of the light, might well have been mistaken for the fingers of the devotee going swiftly through decade after decade of his rosary. [P. 34.]

The action is incomplete. Wing has not, as he hoped, met George Willard; he has understood nothing of himself—his story has been one in which the narrator allows the reader to understand what Wing is, not what Wing will become. A new image of Wing is provided, one which encapsulates him by analogy and by the timeless quality of the image itself—for it is no longer Wing in front of us but the image of a priest engaged in an act that has endured for centuries and that has overtones of the ultimate meaning of eternity. The actual termination is more boldly new, resting on the discovery that terminal effects may be gained from very familiar devices thrust into new positions. Analogies are constant aspects of a work, but to restrict oneself to a single conceit, and to spend that at the end, is to realize how widespread the potential for termination is, how little is actually required to imply termination, and how the feeling of termination may be evoked without reference to the story's central problem, its main action.

The structure of "Hands" is, of course, not the standard for the rest of *Winesburg, Ohio*. Most of the other stories are conventional, commonly beginning with an exposition of character, a few inserts that have determined a character's situation, and culminating with an attempt by the character to meet either George Willard or someone else so that the character could unburden himself of his life story. The attempt usually ends in failure, with Alice Hindman crawling naked on hands and knees back to her house ("Adventure"), or Elmer Cowley pounding on George at the railroad station, then taking the train out of town ("Queer"). And in Anderson's collections outside of *Winesburg*, conventional patterns also predominate. But in many of the stories for which Anderson is best known—"Death in the Woods" (1926) is a good example—linear effects are minimized, and the narrator's building of a story is foregrounded. The story is less a sequence of facts as they happen than an attempt to show the mind at work, trying to make sense of a puzzling image. For the teller of "Death in the Woods" this image is the recollection of a scene he saw in his youth, a "picture there in the forest, the men standing about, the naked girlish-looking figure, face down in the snow, the tracks made by the running dogs and the clear cold Winter sky above."[3] As in "Hands," there are conventional segments of linear suspense; the reader wonders what will happen when the dogs follow the weary Mrs. Grimes, who weakens, waits, can no longer go on. But the story is not what "happened"—the narrator can reconstruct that only by guesswork. The conventional narrative is his invention; the story is the narrator's discovery of the changing meaning of that image for him, until he finally comes to see it as a tableau revealing the way Mrs. Grimes was consumed feeding animal life. Terminating stories of this type is not as difficult as "Hands," for the conclusion the narrator draws about his experience acts as the moral.

Since "Hands" is largely an isolated case of innovation, An-

derson should probably not be regarded as the conscious dis-
coverer of a new pattern designed to achieve closure of form
without closing the action. Anderson has been characterized as
a continuer of the mock oral tradition, in which the narrator's
inability to complete the tale is part of the artifice.[4] Furthermore, Anderson might have genuinely meant those invoca-
tions to a storyteller in "Hands"; he may never have realized
that the device was precisely what allowed him to conceal the
extent of his innovation. Anderson's plea for a storyteller to
tell his story in "Hands," though efficiently disguising the
novelty of his method, should not be taken as pure artifice,
especially in light of his comments in *A Story Teller's Story,* in
which in a passage not coincidentally addressed to hands Anderson pleads: "I talked to my hands, made them promises,
pled with them" to help him learn to write a new way, to get
rid of plot and develop a new form.[5]

Perhaps no one expressed doubt about Anderson's technical
mastery of closure more accurately than Gertrude Stein, writing about *Many Marriages,* a criticism all the more pungent
because it is addressed to Anderson by a critic who was customarily supportive of him: "There is to my thinking a little
too much tendency to make the finale come too frequently
that is to say you the writer know a little too frequently that
there is an ending. May I say that there should be a beginning a
middle and an ending, and you have a tendency to make it a
beginning an ending an ending and an ending."[6] Coming
from anyone else, one might suspect the critic of merely accus-
ing Anderson of failing to use conventional patterns. But
however new a form is, there is still only one ending. What
Stein may have understood in Anderson was his general formlessness, in part innovative, in part simply undisciplined.
Whether or not Anderson knew what he was doing, he created
a form that would allow him, in some of his short stories, to
close on something other than death or annihilation. And yet
to call this form fully "open" is not altogether accurate. All

that remains for Wing is a habitual act, one that if not "dead" is at least "deadening."

Porter, "Flowering Judas"

Katherine Anne Porter was more firmly in control of her craft than was Anderson; her fastidiousness and the consequent diminution of her total output are legendary. Consequently, we might expect her to be more conscious of closure, and her comments on endings and their relation to structure have a familiar ring: "If I didn't know the ending of a story, I wouldn't begin. I always write my last lines, my last paragraph, my last page first, and then I go back and work towards it. I know where I'm going. I know what my goal is."[7] "Flowering Judas" (1930) was clearly a story she had in mind when referring to endings; in the same interview just quoted she mentions it as the one case when her expectations were denied: "In the vision of death at the end of 'Flowering Judas' I knew the real ending—that she was not going to be able to face her life, what she'd done. And I knew that the vengeful spirit was going to come in a dream to tow her away into death, but I didn't know until I'd written it that she was going to wake up saying, 'No!' and be afraid to go to sleep again."[8]

Despite the resemblance of her method of aiming for the end to Poe's method, her stories bear little structural resemblance to his. She does not commonly write a linear, direct story; her technique in "Flowering Judas," like Anderson's, is characterized by a controlling central image (Braggioni sitting before Laura, playing his guitar), and although the image implies pressure and anticipates release, it does not suggest normal narrative sequence.

The departure from traditional form in "Flowering Judas" is what has caught the attention of most critics. Beverly Gross, for instance, has argued that "there is no beginning, middle

and end in this story; there is only a deepening awareness."
"Narrative energy," she argues, is subordinated to "poetic
evocation of a state of mind." The final paragraph is thus "less
a denouement than a synthesizing image." David Madden sees
the structure of the story as a wheel, with the image of Braggioni in Laura's room at the hub and the other incidents arranged as spokes.[9] These nonlinear views of the story are
reasonable when one thinks of "Flowering Judas" in relation to
its nineteenth-century predecessors. Porter does not seem to
rely on an extensive action or movement from point to point
or return, as, for instance, Hawthorne did by beginning
"Roger Malvin's Burial" in the wilderness, then drawing Reuben back to the same spot eighteen years later. Furthermore,
the climax of the story may seem blurred. When Braggioni
exits, his leaving is a false ending—the story continues past it,
actually ending with a dream of Eugenio and Laura's awakening.

Nevertheless, it is profitable to look at the story in the terms
used so far. A problem is immediately identifiable: the initial
image of Braggioni heaped in a chair, singing to Laura in her
bedroom, and Laura, resenting the need to listen to him play
his guitar, avoiding her house until the last possible moment
(Braggioni has appeared every night for two months) is a
tableau that demands resolution. Either Braggioni will satisfy
his needs and cease his caterwauling, or she will rid herself of
him and sleep in peace.

The difference between this and nineteenth-century narrative lies in the way the problem level controls what follows.
Laura devises resolutions in response to her needs, and these
are disposed in a logical array that constitutes a mental equivalent of a developing action. This array of potential resolutions
carries the suggestion of linear movement, though in fact the
resolutions end in indecision, and in that sense movement
seems circular. The original image is simply deepening in its
irony, not progressing toward resolution, thus creating the
illusion of motionlessness.

One consequence of the transfer of movement from action to thought is that endings seem constantly imminent. Laura's first proposed ending is simply to lie down and ignore Braggioni, a form of wish fulfillment. She thinks only briefly of this solution and then asks Braggioni to sing, thus initiating the nightly recurrence of the tableau. Why she does so is explained at least on the simple level—no one crosses Braggioni, no one would "lay a finger on the vast cureless wound of his self-esteem."[10] Laura proposes a tentative explanation of the significance of the scene, thinking of Braggioni in his "gluttonous bulk" as "a symbol of her many disillusions" (p. 91), an explanation that accounts for him but not for her own part in the tableau.

Her next "ending" is the culmination of these unpleasant thoughts—she longs to "fly out of this room" (p. 92), leaving Braggioni to sing by himself, and, because no longer present, she would no longer need to account for herself. This aspiration immediately vanishes, as did her first wish: "Instead she looks at Braggioni" (p. 92). What follows is an explication that sums up the incongruities of the situation, deepening the irony of the second, nonnarrative level. Laura's background, her Roman Catholic upbringing, her fascination with lace, contradict her revolutionary fervor and make the tableau seem all the more incongruous. Matched with the description of her is that of Braggioni, dressed in yellow and purple, his belt "buckled cruelly around his gasping middle." He swells with an "ominous ripeness" (p. 112), as if he were fruit on a tree ready to drop, perhaps a reference to the tree of the story's title. The ominousness is part of a building pressure in the story, pushing toward a bursting point. This pressure is not the result of plot, but it produces an equivalent suspense.

As Braggioni talks to her he introduces an idea that Laura does not understand: "We are more alike than you realize in some things" (p. 93), he claims. The statement evokes in Laura "a slow chill," a "sense of danger," an anticipation of "a shock-

ing death" that waits for her with "lessening patience." His
assertion offers a new meaning for the tableau, one that accounts for her as well as him, contrary to the distancing she
would choose to practice. She tentatively accepts this in spite
of herself—"It may be true I am as corrupt, in another way, as
Braggioni . . . as callous, as incomplete." The conception reduces her to immobility: "She sits quietly, she does not run"
(p. 93). More of her past is introduced, initially with the theme
of her revolutionary activities but blending them with a relation of two courtships, one with a captain who had been a
soldier in Zapata's army and another with a shock-haired
youth who sings to her on her patio by the scarlet blossoms of
the Judas tree. The soldier she escapes by spurring her horse at
an opportune moment; but the youth she has thrown a flower,
on the advice of her maid. These incidents generalize Braggioni's significance; he seems another manifestation of Laura's
more general dilemma. This summary of her past concludes
with the lesson that she draws from all her activities: the power
of the talismanic word "no," a word that appropriately characterizes both the temporary, stalled position of Laura in her
current relation with Braggioni and her more general stagnation. The story seems nowhere closer to not ending at all—as if
it were an archetypal indirect story—than at any other point.

But ironically, when nothing seems likely to happen, the
tension breaks. If all of Laura's proposals to herself are false
endings, the most false ending comes now when Braggioni,
for no particular reason, asks Laura if she is going to sleep.
What follows divides into two parts: the oiling of Braggioni's
pistol and then the tying up of the remaining threads, Braggioni returning to his wife and Laura preparing for sleep, one
of the conventional forms of natural termination. Read for its
overtones, as a Freudian message, the pistol scene is a parody
of resolution. Braggioni is enabled to disrobe at least partially,
unbuckling his ammunition belt. While she cleans and oils, he
advises her that no woman need go begging for satisfaction—

even "the legless beggar woman in the Alameda has a perfectly faithful lover" (p. 100). Braggioni does not get what he came for, but he leaves with his pistol oiled. Then, by accounting for a final reconciliation scene between Braggioni and his wife, Porter provides closure for him; putting Laura to bed by herself should at least get her what she has wanted from the beginning of the story.

Closure underlines not how much but rather how little has been accomplished. One question remains: Braggioni's coming and going has been a meaningful experience for Laura, but in what sense has she been altered by her understanding of him? The question is answered in the last paragraph, not by Laura's consciousness but by her unconscious self, as her thoughts of a character named Eugenio lead to a dream:

> Eat these flowers, poor prisoner, said Eugenio in a voice of pity, take and eat: and from the Judas tree he stripped the warm bleeding flowers and held them to her lips. She saw that his hand was fleshless, a cluster of small white petrified branches, and his eye sockets were without light, but she ate the flowers greedily for they satisfied both hunger and thirst. Murderer! said Eugenio, and Cannibal! This is my body and my blood. Laura cried No! and at the sound of her own voice, she awoke trembling, and was afraid to sleep again. [Pp. 101–2.]

Instead of lapsing into sleep, into natural termination, Laura is left wide awake, trembling. She experiences more disequilibrium than she did when the story opened. Furthermore, Eugenio, who had been a minor character throughout, now appears in a puzzling role. A communion is shockingly inverted, and Laura's hunger, both literal and spiritual, is unfulfilled. Readers, however, expect closure and will search for equilibrium.

To some extent resolution is possible. One can, for example, reconstruct the role of Eugenio. Initially he appears in a passage in which Laura reflects on how she feels herself "caught immovably in this hour, with herself transfixed, Braggioni singing on forever, and Eugenio's body not yet discovered by the guard" (p. 99). Why his body should concern her is revealed later when we learn that he has taken an overdose of the narcotic tablets she brought him and so killed himself. Eugenio serves two contradictory functions (and for that reason he may appear as a curious amalgam in the dream, as man and tree, as savior and accuser): he is, on the one hand, similar to Laura, like her, a prisoner of Braggioni, bored, unwilling to wait for Braggioni to set him free; on the other hand, he is her victim. She has killed him by giving him the narcotics. In this sense it is she who plays the role of Braggioni, who himself is a betrayer of his country as well as its savior, a Judas as much as a Christ. Insofar as Laura is linked to Braggioni, Braggioni's assertion of their identity is fulfilled. The attribution of new significance to phrases as well as solutions to puzzles such as the meaning of the dream of Eugenio might satisfy some of the reader's desire for order and balance, but we could question whether they redress the essential instability. Has the dream, for instance, changed Laura?

Probably not. The dominant word of the ending is still "no," occurring three times in the paragraph before the quoted passage and once in the passage itself. Leon Gottfried has provided a compelling analysis, based on the story's allusions to Dante, of Laura as a character in limbo, permanently fixed in inaction, and this characterization of her is not changed by her posture at the end.[11]

Even so, we should note that Laura has been "awakened." She may no more change her ways than Wakefield might, but Porter has ended her story with the suggestion that Laura's unconscious is at least at work, sending her messages. No integration of her personality is predicted, but there is not, as in Hawthorne's "Wakefield," a narrative voice declaring the impossibility of alteration.

In sum, the reader can sense stability but not total balance.

The structure creates a syncopated effect, seeming to lead to a close before the story is over, then opening up again. The sense of negation, the trembling and fear of the final sentence, suspend the ending, and the dual attitude the reader might have toward Laura's change complements this suspension. Laura is fixed in her attitudes, but the reader can see, even if she cannot, the process of change potentially at work. In nineteenth-century stories such as "Bartleby the Scrivener," the reader is also responsible for holding in suspension several themes— guilt and responsibility, for instance—but natural termination and encapsulation round off a straightforward structure, as if the writer could not risk raising unsettling moral issues until he had provided the reader with a structurally closed experience.

Nineteenth-century stories that end on a note of uncertainty do, to be sure, exist: witness Hawthorne's "My Kinsman, Major Molineux." After Robin's ambiguous outburst of laughter directed at his kinsman during the symbolic parricide of tar and feathers, celebrated by onlookers with "counter-feited pomp, in senseless uproar, in frenzied merriment, trampling all on an old man's heart" (11:230), Hawthorne adds a touch that opens up the story. Robin wants to go home, to leave town to return to his village—"Will you show me the way to the ferry?" (p. 231) he repeats—but the gentleman with him defers showing him, suggesting to Robin that he rise in the world without the help of his kinsman. We never learn whether Robin chooses his own village and consequently stagnation or an urban American destiny ambiguously short on decorum and stability.

Robin's experience is left as undetermined as Laura's in "Flowering Judas"; the gentleman's tap on his shoulder has awakened him from a dreamlike state and left him with a major moral choice. The difference, however, is the effect of this openness on the rest of the story. By placing the climax so near the end and by bringing back the cast of characters whom

Robin met earlier, Hawthorne creates a traditional, formally balanced pattern. Though different from the dominant expectation of total closure common in a direct story of this period, the open ending is an isolated effect with no structural consequences for the work as a whole. Not until the twentieth century do we see suspension thoroughly worked into the structure of a story, and not until the twentieth century does this openness become almost a norm, which the reader expects in a story that identifies itself as modern.

Compressed Form

Hemingway, "Cat in the Rain," "Hills Like White Elephants," "The Short Happy Life of Francis Macomber"

In contrast to the imagist form of "Hands" and "Flowering Judas," fashioned by small loops wound around a basically static image, Hemingway's stories characteristically have no loops; instead, time flows forward without interruption. The time span is very short, and the problem level (the subject or theme) either develops very slowly or is presented obliquely, symbolically. These omissions affect both the ending and the anticipation of direct movement toward a goal and thus alter the structure of the story as a whole.

The compressed form may be regarded as a modernized version of the direct form, depending even more heavily on the original goals of direct form, singleness and compression. The essential innovation of the direct form, starting a story closer to the end, was one step toward this tightness. Stories by Poe and Hawthorne seem compact more because of consistency of mood than because of restrictions in situation or time. Though the mood of destruction hangs over "The Fall of the House of Usher," the actual destruction takes at least a week; "Roger Malvin's Burial" takes eighteen years. Stories by Hawthorne and Poe that span a single night, "Young Goodman Brown" and "The Pit and the Pendulum," for instance, feature nightmarish stretches supernaturally charged, hallucinated beyond the normal sense of time. Stories restricted in the classic direct fashion customarily deal with heightened moments, times of extreme emotion or stress, in contrast to stories in the compressed form, which present more ordinary moments.

Stories in the direct form with tendencies toward compression are essentially what Henry James rejected as unworkable, the form of a "detached incident, single and sharp, as clear as a pistol-shot." The compressed story of the twentieth century is not foreshortened after the fashion James practiced; it does not condense a longer tale or a longer time period into a short telling. Foreshortened in an altogether different fashion, the form highlights an incident small and slight in itself, presenting it so that the reader must imagine a much larger context. The incident selected would be so deepened by implied extensions as to suggest both the past and the future, thus equaling the range of a story spanning a much longer time. The complexity or continuity that James longed for was out of the story, not in it, and in this way the compressed form, in relying on the reader to reconstruct the implied story, depends, like the image form, on the reader's awareness of conventional narrative expectations for its full effect. The advantage of the form is that the writer can achieve the goal that eluded James, brevity with fullness; the disadvantage, that the form can become highly ambiguous, the original intention essentially unrecoverable.

The writer most clearly identified with the compressed technique is Hemingway, and he illustrates the power as well as the penalties of the form. Not all of his stories are compressed—it is a characteristic primarily of his early fiction. In many of the later stories, he returned, much as James had, to more conventional structure and closural devices. In the 1938 collection of his first forty-nine stories, the first four, as he points out in the preface, were the last four he had written, and three of them, "The Short Happy Life of Francis Macomber" (1936), "The Capital of the World" (1936), and "The Snows of Kilimanjaro" (1936), end with the deaths of their protagonists, the most conventional form of natural termination. Macomber has his brains blown out by his wife; Paco is gored by a "bull" that is actually a chair with meat knives bound to its legs; and Harry may think he is going to the top of Kilimanjaro, "great, high, and unbelievably white in the sun," but his wife cannot make him answer and his breathing has stopped.[12] The writer who could get so much out of so little comes to depend, like James in his final stories, as surely as Poe had, on death to complete his stories. Rather than discuss these stories, I will concentrate on the earlier ones and then consider the problem of ending in "The Short Happy Life of Francis Macomber," a more conventional direct story.

In defining his primary goal in writing the short story, Hemingway repeatedly used the analogy of an iceberg, an appropriate metaphor for the compressed form. The story the reader sees is only what floats on the surface; beneath is the story the writer has implied. "If a writer of prose knows enough about what he is writing about," he argued, the writer "may omit things that he knows and the reader, if the writer is writing truly enough, will have a feeling of those things as strongly as though the writer had stated them."[13]

One item the writer writing truly enough might omit, apparently, was the ending. In *A Moveable Feast* Hemingway claimed to have omitted "the real end" of "Out of Season" (1923), "which was that the old man hanged himself."[14] Unfortunately, no known readers have ever surmised that the old man, Peduzzi, does hang himself; such an interpretation seems entirely unjustified. Peduzzi, flushed with the thought that he will be able to serve as a guide and will no longer have to make a living by "breaking up frozen manure with a dung fork" (p. 179), should certainly be depressed by the brush-off from the young gentleman, who does not want him as guide for a proposed fishing trip the next day, but nothing in the story suggests suicidal tendencies in Peduzzi. What Hemingway seems to have meant by omitting the ending is that he left out the circumstance that led to the writing of the story—the guide who served as a model for Peduzzi did commit suicide.[15]

Whatever Hemingway's intent, endings in the conventional nineteenth-century sense are largely absent in the compressed form as he used it. He clearly rejected surprise endings. As he commented in *Death in the Afternoon,* the "wow" at the end would be "de trop"; "it is years," he maintained, "since I added the wow to the end of a story."[16] He also avoided endings in the tradition of the direct form, with the various thematic, symbolic, and dramatic aspects coming to a simultaneous close, summarily dismissing the method of the Poe story: "It is skillful, marvellously constructed, and it is dead."[17] Hemingway's endings are not the goal toward which all of the story is clearly directed. More typically stories imply incompleteness—Ole Andreson in "The Killers" (1927), for instance, still waits in his room for his assassins to appear.

The variety of unexpected effects he achieves with his endings is virtually a trademark of a Hemingway story. "The Doctor and the Doctor's Wife" (1924) concludes with Nick—who has played no role, even as witness, to his father's quarrel with Dick Boulton or the discussion between the doctor and his wife—announcing that he knows where some squirrels are. The doctor then replies, "Let's go there" (p. 103), ending the story by a simple exit. When a story seems to have come to its conclusion naturally, as with Marjorie in "The End of Something" (1925) leaving after learning that Nick no longer finds love "any fun," Hemingway goes on a bit longer by having Nick's friend Bill appear and then ends with Bill getting a sandwich and having "a look at the rods" (p. 111). In "The End of Something," instead of omitting the end, Hemingway seems to have gone beyond the actual endpoint. A device that might normally have closural force is inverted in "A Clean, Well-Lighted Place" (1933): the old waiter goes home to sleep but knows he will be unable to until dawn; the emphasis is more on sleeplessness than sleep.[18]

When a story does end on a firm and positive resolution, the resolution is almost inevitably ironic. At the end of "Indian Camp" (1924), Nick, having witnessed the death of the Indian whose child was being born in the bunk below, is "quite sure that he would never die" (p. 95); "Mr. and Mrs. Elliot" (1924—not a compressed story but at least a brief tale) ends with the narrator asserting that "they were all quite happy" (p. 164). Nick will come to understand death a great deal more precisely in later stories, and the menage à trois the Elliots have concocted cannot end well; Mr. Elliot has moved to another bedroom, has taken to drinking white wine, and after laboring over his poetry, emerges in the morning looking "very exhausted."

Irony in these cases creates a sense of openness. Taken literally, the statement of absoluteness carries finality; at the same time, the ironic undertone suggests that the central problem is still unresolved. Structurally the stories are closed; thematically they are not. Two stories in particular, "Cat in the Rain" and "Hills Like White Elephants," illustrate the process in more detail, and they show the difficulties inherent in the form.

The wife in "Cat in the Rain" (1925) gets what she wants, a cat, and such a resolution to the action of the overt problem would normally bring a story to a full close. The issue, however, is whether the reader can accurately assemble the information that has been provided. There is first the problem of whether the cat she gets is the one she wants. The cat she originally saw was not identified; the reader knows only that it tried to crouch under a table to keep out of the rain and that in doing so it kept itself "compact." She speaks of it, with her husband, as a "kitty" (p. 167), a term that seems accurate until the ending calls it into question. What she actually gets is a "big tortoise-shell cat" (p. 170) that swings down against the body of the maid who brings it, a much larger animal than a kitty that would "sit on my lap and purr when I stroke her" (p. 169), as the wife had earlier imagined. If it is not the cat she wanted, the wife will be disillusioned. The one thing she wanted, if she could not have all the other things—long hair, silver, and candles—was a cat, and she will not even get the cat she wants. If it is the cat she originally saw, however, she has deluded herself into imagining that the cat is something other than what it is, and she is not likely to be satisfied.

Because of the associations that range around the cat through the development of the story, whether the cat is the one she wanted has other consequences. The cat has been sent by the padrone, whom she much admires; he seems to possess the masculine protectiveness her husband lacks. If the cat is the one she saw, the padrone has been far more thoughtful than her husband, who simply lies on his bed and reads. If, however, it is simply any cat the padrone could supply, his officiousness and eagerness to please will be of no more use to her than her husband, who ignores her entirely.[19]

The ending of the story is not so problematic as this analysis suggests; all of these versions point in the same direction. Whether the cat is the same one and whether the padrone has been genuinely perceptive and helpful do not matter a great deal. The actual cat is not going to be what she expected; no cat would bring her the satisfaction she wants. No simple object can by displacement fulfill all the needs she must suppress. Were the story a fairy tale, we would consider her a character who has made a foolish wish, the fulfillment of which will not achieve its goal.

"Hills Like White Elephants" (1927) departs more insistently from standard narrative form than does "Cat in the Rain," and consequently it illustrates better how compressed form alters narrative structure. In compressed form the slow revelation of theme is almost an identifying characteristic. The forward pressure that normally drives the reader to seek a resolution to the problem presented in the opening is replaced by the drive to find the problem, the thematic center. At the beginning of "Hills Like White Elephants" all that is obvious is the dissension between the man and the woman. A simple remark that the hills look like white elephants sets them to bickering:

> "I've never seen one," the man drank his beer.
> "No, you wouldn't have."
> "I might have," the man said. "Just because you say I wouldn't have doesn't prove anything." [P. 273.]

The woman quickly shifts the topic, and they return to a totally unemotional question-and-response conversation. The pattern of sudden outbursts followed by equally sudden returns to equanimity sets up a tension in the formal sense of an expectation of repetition, while also inviting the reader to construct his own idea of the relationship between them. After bickering erupts again around her remark that everything one waits for tastes of licorice, the central problem is revealed (although obliquely): the man's desire for the woman to have a "simple operation," one "just to let the air in" (p. 275).

To replace the traditional expectation of an ending deriving from an immediately disclosed problem Hemingway commonly supplies a supporting action that carries its own predicted ending. Hemingway frequently introduces a natural event with its own resolution early in the story, and even though this event is not the story's primary focus, it serves to suggest a traditional end-predicting structure. In the case of "Hills Like White Elephants," there are two such devices—the arrival of the train and the drinking of beer. The first paragraph of the story informs the reader that the train from Barcelona is due in forty minutes. If nothing else, its arrival will end the conversation between the man and woman who wait for it.

Hemingway does not end the story with the train's arrival (or with the beers consumed); the man, having moved their bags, looks up the tracks and goes back to talk to the woman. The actual arrival, true to the iceberg analogy, does not need to be in the story.

Although the problem level is slow to develop, it clearly exists and requires resolution. Hemingway here gives the story a unique turn: the problem does not appear to be resolved, and in that sense the story has no ending. The woman in particular would simply like to stop talking about the issue. "Would you please please please please please please please stop talking?" she requests, after which the man, of course, talks once more, and the woman responds, "I'll scream" (p. 277). But what Hemingway implies about the future of the characters and the way he secures a sense of completion do provide closure. These are characters whose future is not promising: "We could have everything and every day we make it more impossible" (p. 276), the woman says, melodramatically to be sure, but accurately assessing their probable future. Their discussion has pushed them further apart, not closer together. We know enough about each of them to understand how unlikely it is that they will resolve their problems and stay together. We know the man largely through his clichés about naturalness, happiness, and simplicity, mixed with his inability to hear what he says—"I'm perfectly willing to go through with it if it means anything to you" (p. 277), he maintains, though he cannot stop talking about not going through with it. He claims, "I don't want anybody but you," a cliché that might make sense if the discussion were about leaving her, and thus "anybody" would be another woman, but the "anybody" in this case is their unborn child, and although his claim appears on the surface to be one of fidelity it is in fact one of selfishness and irresponsibility. We know as well the woman's attitude, her tendency to alternate "I don't care about me" (p. 276) with the implied annoyance of not being cared about enough, as well as her desire to close discussion of the issue.

One word suffices to demonstrate how fixed the man has
become in his attitude at the end, the word "reasonably" in the
line "They were all waiting reasonably for the train." The rest
of the paragraph refers only to the man's physical actions as he
returns to the barroom and sees others waiting. He "looked at
them," and then "he went out" (p. 278). Only the words "reasonably waiting" give a clue to his thoughts. They suggest that
he thinks all the others wait reasonably, but he is stuck with an
unreasonable woman. That is the sum of his evaluation of the
discussion: he has learned nothing.

Agreement between the characters that their problem has
been resolved is not required for closure. Our realization as
readers that we have seen enough to form a judgment, to
understand the situation, is sufficient. We do not need to learn
more to predict the course of events. This realization, however, is external to the story and still leaves the writer with the
responsibility of signaling by other means that the story is
over. The relations must appear to stop somewhere. This task
does not prove to be especially difficult, and it is achieved in
"Hills" by a form of natural termination used ironically. The
final lines of the story, "'I feel fine,' she said. 'There's nothing
wrong with me. I feel fine'" (p. 278), are terminal in several
senses. They assert well-being that in itself can terminate a
story, and they strategically preclude further conversation.
The repetition also suggests irony, and irony has its own
closural force at the antithetical level. Instead of traversing
space, this story covers a range of emotional attitudes. Termination on an ironic expression has a stability of its own, for it
suggests the ultimate poles of an experience, limits beyond
which no further exploration is either possible or required.

The writer who depends on the reader to deal with these
ironies and to complete the story assumes certain risks. Commonly the ending in all traditions has a special purpose, giving
final shape to the story and resolving ambiguities that have
kept the reader in suspense. The reader can discern the path
among the thicket of turns that have confronted him all along.

Endings of compressed stories, however, or any stories with a low rate of redundancy, may not always work as the writer might hope. Ambiguities the writer has woven into a rich texture may lose their design in the fabric. Errors and uncertainties gain in magnitude. "Cat in the Rain" is on the edge of the problem; "The Short Happy Life of Francis Macomber," although not a compressed story, demonstrates the consequences of these risks.

Interpretation of the ending of "Macomber," called "Happy Ending" when it first appeared in *Cosmopolitan* in 1936, has divided most readers into two camps. Arthur Waldhorn and Carlos Baker consider Wilson a reliable commentator on the action of the story; in Baker's words, Wilson is "the standard of manhood toward which Macomber rises."[20] They share Wilson's assumption that Margot Macomber shot her husband because she feared losing him and because she could not risk the anticipated consequences of his new freedom and courage. Others, most notably Warren Beck and Virgil Hutton, do not trust Wilson's account and believe that he abuses Margaret in the final scene; Hutton calls Wilson "the butt rather than the spokesman of Hemingway."[21]

Although in one sense the ending is fundamentally closed, with Macomber dead, the short happy life of his momentary courage gained in the buffalo-hunting episode over, the significance of his wife's act is clearly still undetermined. There is very little that one can be sure of, and not everyone agrees about that. Did, for instance, Mrs. Macomber literally shoot at her husband? We are told that Mrs. Macomber "had shot at the buffalo with the 6.5 Mannlicher as it seemed about to gore Macomber" by a narrator whose authority we have no reason to question. She shot at the buffalo, not at Macomber.[22] Even if the gun she used was not appropriate for killing the buffalo, and even if its name is symbolic of Margot's intentions, the narrator claims she shot at the buffalo. Resolution of this particular issue, however, would not necessarily advance our understanding of the story. Even if she did not mean to kill her husband, it seems equally undeniable that throughout the story her whole being is in opposition to his and her act is an inevitable consequence. Unconsciously she must kill him. She lives only when Macomber weakens; when Macomber regains his courage she grows frightened and pale. The only end to their vampire relationship, which seems in some ways straight out of Poe, is for her to eliminate him. Some critics have tried to defend Margot, arguing that she is, or will be, repentant—Beck argues that before the end she ruminates not on revenge but on her shame and defeat; furthermore, "if she had wanted him dead, she could have left it to the buffalo." Anne Greco argues that Margot plays the bitch in order to startle Macomber into atonement.[23]

Neither of these arguments seems convincing; Margot plays the role of "enamelled bitch" too thoroughly in word and action to be excused from the consequences, and any thought of her role-playing is merely hopeful surmise, particularly dubious because Hemingway has been unusually explicit about the thoughts and intentions of each character, and nowhere does he show her considering pretense. Readings that humanize her create a more open-ended story but one that rests more on the critic's standard of human behavior than on encouragement from the text.

Wilson's role is even more difficult to gauge. To many critics the ending must be read as the vindication of the code of masculinity. John Hill treats Wilson as Hemingway's spokesman and argues that in the ending Wilson "beats down" Margaret, forcing her to say "please," because he "will not see Francis's victory wasted."[24] Margaret is seen as a bitch who must be brought to her knees. To other critics Wilson is no paragon of masculine virtue—his illegal dependence on a car during the chase taints his heroic pose, his treatment of the natives is cruel, and his use of Mrs. Macomber in the cot may, as Hutton and Beck argue, be manly but is greedily opportunistic. Seen this way, his motive in humbling Margot is ignoble; she has tales to tell about him, and he now has the chance to bludgeon her into silence.

It would be easy to say that Hemingway wants to leave open the matter of whether Margot intended to kill her husband, but I share the judgment of R. S. Crane: if "'suspension of judgment' about the cause of Macomber's death is the intended final state of mind of the reader, then Hemingway has bungled his job."[25] Readers have sought in the ending a vindication of one particular principle—either proper masculine dominance on the part of Wilson, imposing himself on Margot as Francis should have, or the imminent self-realization of Mrs. Macomber—but I do not believe Hemingway has given the reader clear signals. If he meant us to appreciate Macomber's masculinity, he was blind to Wilson's shortcomings and has, to use Crane's terms, simply bungled. A close analysis of this ending suggests that the reader can interpret the story only by ignoring elements that do not fit his presuppositions. Stories of this sort, I would argue, are not so much open-ended as badly constructed.

CHAPTER 6

The Twentieth Century: Extending the Frame

The Illusion of Openness

Oates, "Where Are You Going, Where Have You Been," and Capote, "Miriam"

Hemingway's iceberg analogy provides an image for the reader's construction of a story larger than the one that appears on the surface. Taken literally, however, the image suggests something looming vertically underneath rather than extending horizontally along the surface. Translated into terms of a story, the image suggests that the additional dimension supplied by the reader is internal, a matter of depth and significance, and not, for instance, an enlarged time span before or after the story.

The limits of the metaphor seem to match the limits of Hemingway's practice. Time is implied before the couple sat down at the train station in "Hills," and time is implied afterward, but the reader is not forced to imagine either. Rather, Hemingway strives to convince us that we do not need to know more. Slight as the incident may be, it tells us all we need. The iceberg is thus underneath, expressed as depth and compression.

Many stories by other writers that seem to open up, imply-

119

ing time beyond the frame of the story, also do not encourage the reader to extend beyond the endpoint. The open ending, particularly in modern terror stories—Joyce Carol Oates's "Where Are You Going, Where Have You Been?" (1966) and Truman Capote's "Miriam" (1944) are examples—is largely a convention. In these stories gothic trimmings are initially suppressed in favor of realism, a concession that serves first to disguise the form and ultimately to heighten its effects.

Both "Where Are You Going" and "Miriam" start with the commonplace, with Oates's Connie left at home while her parents go to a barbecue, and Capote's Mrs. H. T. Miller alone in a "pleasant apartment (two rooms with kitchenette) in a remodeled brownstone near the East River."[1] Both have visitors. Connie's is a fifteen-year-old fellow with "shaggy black hair" and metallic, mirroring sunglasses, whom she has seen only once before at a drive-in, when he wagged his finger at her and said, "Gonna get you, baby."[2] Mrs. Miller's visitor is a young girl with silver-white hair and a "tailored plum-velvet coat" (p. 18), who asks Mrs. Miller to buy her a movie ticket, then later finds her apartment. Oates's visitor is a punk version of Emily Dickinson's gentleman caller, his carriage a "convertible jalopy painted gold" (p. 37); when she leaves with "vast sunlit reaches of land behind," she too is beginning to surmise where she is headed, toward land that she "had never seen before and did not recognize except to know that she was going to it" (p. 54). Mrs. Miller is at the mercy of a wickedly precocious Miriam, who takes a cameo brooch, eats food that is offered her—"ravenously, and when the sandwiches and milk were gone, her fingers made cobweb movements over the plate, gathering crumbs" (p. 23). When defied, the girl hurls a vase filled with paper roses to the floor. The announcement that Miriam has come to live with her leaves Mrs. Miller no more pleased than she would be to find a devil proposing to perch itself at the foot of her bed. The fact that a neighbor investigates the apartment for her and finds no one only increases the impact when Mrs. Miller returns to hear the sound of a bureau opening and closing, until it was

> replaced by the murmur of a silk dress and this, delicately faint, was moving nearer and nearer and swelling in intensity till the walls trembled with the vibration and the room was caving under a wave of whispers. Mrs. Miller stiffened and opened her eyes to a dull, direct stare.
> "Hello," said Miriam.[P. 30.]

Oates and Capote have modernized their gothic tales, shifting the focus somewhat from the horror that invades the lives of these woman to a psychological study of supposedly normal but proud and narrow people who believe they have arranged the world securely to meet their needs only to confront unexpectedly larger and more savage futures. In these stories Capote and Oates have intensified the effect, not with the hammering and stylized diction of Poe but with striking contrasts, to the very end, between the ordinary and the dreaded. These stories are firmly in the "Ligeia" tradition, emphasizing by slow and steady linear progression and inevitable close an ending that seems to open into what is in one case the gaining of a child, the acceptance of a date, into the visitation of an incubus. This is Poe transposed to the modern city apartment or the suburban ranch house. The openness that terminates each story, like the openness at the end of "Ligeia," is largely illusory. Miriam may say the traditional word of beginning, "hello," and Connie may be only beginning a journey, but there is virtually no ambiguity about what is to follow. Readers are encouraged not to imagine continuation but to realize how unimaginable continuation would be. These two endings, along with that of "Ligeia," could be viewed as a special trick of an essentially closed form: the apparent openness of the final sequence, always an emblem of a "new" beginning, is in fact an ironic marker of the extent to which characters are trapped and destroyed by situations they have in part created. They may think themselves free, but they are not.

O'Connor, "Parker's Back"

Before looking at stories that do project the reader beyond the endpoint, we ought to consider another possibility—Flannery O'Connor's "Parker's Back" (1965), which implies continuity even though the formal conditions of closure have been met. O'Connor's stories do not commonly end on open actions; as she has said, they tend to be closed by death: "I can't imagine a story that doesn't properly end in it or its foreshadowings."[3] The endings of her stories, in Ruth M. Vande Kieft's words, characteristically force the reader "from an amused detachment and a partly pleasurable disgust, to a horrified recognition of both the justice and painfulness of what is taking place."[4] "Parker's Back," the last story O'Connor wrote, is nearly the only one that avoids this pattern.

In one sense all that is needed to finish the story is one more tattoo on O.E. (the initials stand for Obadiah Elihue; all but his back has been covered with tattoos when the story starts) and the discovery of whether he has achieved his purpose with his final tattoo. His actions are motivated by a desire, which he does not fully understand, to gain his wife's admiration. The final tattoo will be a symbol that Sarah Ruth "would not be able to resist," so that, as the tattoo artist notes, "she'll like it and lay off you awhile."[5] Despite the glorious Byzantine Christ he selects, Sarah Ruth rejects him. She does not recognize the image, calls him an idolator, and thrashes him with a broom. O.E.'s original goal of pleasing Sarah Ruth seemingly out of reach, and the story in one sense is complete. Parker has failed—instead of admiring his latest tattoo, his wife humiliates him.

In support of the close of the problem level, other closural signals converge. When he whispers his name to make his wife admit him back into his house, and gives it in the form of Obadiah Elihue, the sun bursts over the morning skyline, and he feels "the light pouring through him, turning his spider web soul into a perfect arabesque of colors, a garden of trees and birds and beasts" (p. 528), an image of transfiguration with natural terminal qualities. The final scene is encapsulated by a shift to the point of view of Sarah Ruth, who shakes the broom with which she has just beaten Parker "to get the taint of him off it." Through her eyes we have the final sight of Parker: "There he was—who called himself Obadiah Elihue—leaning against the tree, crying like a baby" (p. 530).

But the story is not really about what O.E. wants and intends to do; it is about what happens to him in spite of his intent. Causality in his mind might be direct, but the reader sees easily that O.E. is constantly manipulated rather than in control of his destiny. This is true not only of the story as a whole but also from moment to moment, as when he thinks he is finished with Sarah Ruth and ends up married to her:

> And as he reached for her, she thrust him away with such force that the door of the truck came off and he found himself flat on his back on the ground. He made up his mind then and there to have nothing further to do with her.
>
> They were married in the Country Ordinary's office because Sarah Ruth thought churches were idolatrous. Parker had no opinion about that one way or the other. The Ordinary's office was lined with cardboard file boxes and record books. [P. 518.]

Preoccupied with minor perceptions, he misses the larger point—he marries the woman he thought he had finished with. Through each step of the story he thinks himself free of his problems, and each step binds him more.

The reader cannot take Sarah Ruth's final view of O.E. as his or her own. God may be a spirit and may not be appropriately represented by the tattoo on Parker's back, as she asserts. But

she cannot see as the reader does how Parker has been pos-
sessed by the figure on his back, how his spider web soul has
been illuminated by the tattoo whose "all-demanding eyes"
(p. 522) command his attention as her "icepick eyes" (p. 524)
never will. She may have humiliated and scourged him, but
she sees no irony in not recognizing the Byzantine Christ on
his back or in having in effect crucified her husband.

O'Connor has set in motion a paradox, has shown a man
mastered by an image that will take him out of his world.
Whenever O.E. thinks he has understood a situation it turns
out to mean something else, and so by analogy his final moment of defeat requires an unstated balance, which can be
fulfilled only in the reader. "Parker's Back" could well be analyzed as a closed story, but the ambiguity of the ending, of the
man who is mastered into a submission he does not yet understand, leaves as a residue an internal openness, a pattern similar
in effect but more obvious in intent to Hawthorne's "Roger
Malvin's Burial"; the paradox of humiliation and vindication
cannot and is not meant to be rationally resolved, and so the
story seems to slip, for all its closed features, beyond the geometry of the telling to a mystery. Structurally a story like
"Parker's Back" does not use closural signals to control the
action of the story any differently from most stories written a
hundred years earlier; the difference is that thematic considerations override them.

The Practice of Openness

Updike, "Ace in the Hole"

Structurally open stories often derive from the pattern Hemingway popularized, the compressed form. Imitations are
abundant—Irwin Shaw's "The Girls in Their Summer
Dresses" (1947) in many ways resembles "Hills Like White
Elephants," and so does John Updike's "Ace in the Hole"

(1955)—and crises faced by young couples seem particularly adaptable to this approach. But Shaw, by closing with the revelation that the husband, Michael, can see his wife only as a sex object, adds the sort of "wow" that Hemingway disdained, and it closes off the story. Until the end the reader was likely to take Michael's side against his querulous wife, but the ending abruptly undercuts our sympathy and implies that, as in "Hills," argumentative positions will irreconcilably harden. Action continues, but by saving a snap for the end, making the reader invert his reading of the story, Shaw enforces completion.

Updike's "Ace in the Hole" can be read as a closed story, but certain elements do open it. In some respects Updike's practice seems conventional; he works with the same end-directedness that characterizes many writers, trying, in his words, "instantly to set in motion a certain forward tilt of suspense or curiosity, and at the end of the story or novel to rectify the tilt, to complete the motion."[6] The change in vocabulary, with the emphasis on the slightness of "tilt," and the barely noticeable correction that "rectify" implies, show how muted these objectives have become.

"Ace in the Hole" begins with the same slow development of the problem level, the same slow exposition that moves from simple to more complex levels of suspense, that characterizes the compressed form. The reader's charge at this point is first to assemble the terms of the conflict. The opening paragraph proposes only a simple problem: "The moment his car touched the boulevard heading home, Ace flicked on the radio. He needed the radio, especially today. In the seconds before the tubes warmed up, he said aloud, doing it just to hear a human voice, 'Jesus. She'll pop her lid.'"[7] While provoking the reader to seek answers to these questions—who is "she," why will she pop her lid?—Updike completes the exposition. The first woman Ace meets, his mother, is evidently not "she," because when his mother finds out that he has lost his job, she responds, "Good for you" (p. 16). The "she" in question turns out to be Ace's wife, Evey. At first, the issue of his having lost his job is dismissed—she has already heard about it, but she flares up and threatens to leave him. She's "fed up" and "ready as Christ to let [him] run" (p. 24). The issue of the job was only a smaller one in the context of her greater dissatisfaction with him.

While working to identify the central problem the reader is also likely to attend to minor questions such as Ace's age. Ace seems at first very young, perhaps still in high school, a drag-racing kid, listening to the radio, flipping his cigarette out the window. Yet when another driver pulls up next to his car, he feels himself old, separated by a "little gap of years," some distance from the kids who are "young and mean and shy" (p. 15). There is a disparity between what he thinks of himself and what his actions suggest about him. He thinks of himself as Ace, but his mother calls him Freddy.

A more significant puzzle for the reader is the complexity of Ace as a character. Despite his obvious immaturity he shows signs of wisdom: he ignores his mother's encouragement to break up his marriage, and although he acted foolishly in the incident (involving parking cars) that got him fired, he is neither proud nor defensive. He regrets leaving his past—his nickname comes from his former status as a high school basketball player—but his hesitation in reading the article his mother has mentioned shows a capacity to move beyond his former self. The slow development of the problem permits the reader to invest interest in character study, and it is this particularity, this interest in social realism, that in part differentiates Updike's approach from Hemingway's.

As the story nears its end, the intensity unobtrusively increases. Ace first raises the stakes, giving the theme of the risk of the marriage a new context. The baby interrupts Evey's angry speech about Ace's "hot-shot stunts" (p. 24) by putting an ashtray on her head, an interruption which Evey, by noting sarcastically that the baby is "cute as her daddy," brings us back to the theme of her anger. Ace then makes a demonstration of his own from the baby, using her grasp of the rattle to illustrate her genetic talent as a potential basketball player, a talent he argues is wasted because she is a girl. What they need is another child. His effort is audacious, for at the point of her readiness to leave, he is angling for another offspring, Fred junior.

The ultimate scene brings into play both the progressive and regressive elements in Ace's character. The scene is announced as terminal by two markers. The first is when Ace turns on the radio (the phrase "before the tubes warmed up" [p. 25] is an exact repetition of a phrase in the third sentence of the opening), which indicates that in a moment of crisis he meets the need by performing this ritual. The second marker is a nirvana theme, used ironically. As he begins to dance with Evey to the music of the radio, "he seemed to be great again, and all the other kids were around them, in a ring, clapping time" (p. 26): he has conjured up the past as a salve to self-esteem, as a way to see himself great again.

The ironic note of the ending stresses his regression: "The music ate through his skin and mixed with the nerves and small veins," and in a druglike state Ace imagines he has won the argument, escaping the strictures of the present. Ace is a boy who will never grow up, a boy who has conceived the unfortunate idea of holding together an impossible marriage solely to replicate himself and has compelled his wife into stunned acquiescence in his dreamy, regressive dance.

But a substratum of the text suggests that Ace's progression cannot be ignored. Unlike the males of the Shaw or Hemingway stories, he wants to sustain a marriage, not to evade or destroy it. His transition to adult life has been difficult, and in the ending he retreats to images of the past. But in this story, unlike the others, the wife is part of the scene he constructs. She has been "seized" to participate in the dance, but what follows does not resemble rape—he fits his hand "into the natural place on Evey's back and she shuffled stiffly into his lead." He spins her out "carefully," and then "her hair brushed his lips as she minced in, then swung away, to the end of his arm; he could feel her toes dig into the carpet." She may know she is being taken in, allowing Ace to shift the topic, to seduce her and to score one more time. But acquiescence here need not mean capitulation ever after. In contrast, "Hills Like White Elephants" does not resolve the quarrel, but thematically the story predicts disaster and separation. The train is coming, closing the scene. The scene in Updike's story is still moving; the dance goes on. Ace's regression at the end may be temporary, and his ability to survive may outweigh the pull backward. He is not, as his mother would like him to be, eager to return to his past as if his present does not exist. His wife's silence, if not shared dreaming, may at least indicate a willingness to stay. The dance is an ambiguous ending, for it can be read both as a close and an opening. Even the title suggests ambiguity—Ace is on the spot, in the hole. Ace may be aiming for another hole, a bedroom hoop. But an ace in the hole is a good card to have, and it can build a winning hand.

Most readers, I suspect, will not want to suspend the ending and will prefer to emphasize Ace's regression. But elements of openness can be ignored only at the cost of the richness of the story. "Ace in the Hole" is typical of the suspension we have come to favor in the short story. The reader will provide a close based on what he or she takes to be the dominant tone, but the suspension is necessary for the final effect. Anything thoroughly closed might not seem modern, might appear to portray life dishonestly.

Malamud, "The Magic Barrel"

Because of the reader's tendency to apply closure even when confronted with contradictions, stories that extend the frame beyond the endpoint more or less require a consistent sense of

THE PRACTICE OF OPENNESS

ambiguity from the outset. Doubleness in Malamud's "The Magic Barrel" (1954), for instance, emerges early. The basic idea of the story is similar to that of "Parker's Back"—Leo Finkle, a young rabbinical student, is in search of a bride. Like O'Connor's boorish and conceited O.E., the lower-class itinerant farm worker who has also avoided religion, Leo will also presumably be brought to marriage and to a level of religious commitment. The treatment, however, is more obviously ambiguous.

Leo at first rejects several prospects offered by the marriage broker, Pinye Salzman, and then settles on the marriage broker's own daughter, Stella. The richness of the story derives partly from the ploys of both the negotiators, Finkel and Salzman, and even more from the double treatment. Salzman may have manipulated Leo's interest in his daughter after all, and his disapproval of the match, on the grounds that his daughter has deserted the faith, may be one more strategy from a man who has exhausted every other attempt to marry off his daughter. Salzman might even be superhuman; his ability to appear on demand makes him seem like a spirit, whether a guardian spirit or a tempter. The final two paragraphs bring Leo to his highly ambiguous match:

> Leo was informed by letter that she would meet him on a certain corner, and she was there one spring night, waiting under a street lamp. He appeared, carrying a small bouquet of violets and rosebuds. Stella stood by the lamp post, smoking. She wore white with red shoes, which fitted his expectations, although in a troubled moment he had imagined the dress red, and only the shoes white. She waited uneasily and shyly. From afar he saw that her eyes—clearly her father's—were filled with desperate innocence. He pictured, in her, his own redemption. Violins and lit candles revolved in the sky. Leo ran forward with flowers outthrust.[8]

Doubleness and opposition recur within the passage, from the alternative distribution of red and white to the oxymoronic phrase "desperate innocence." The stability of the scene is partly a pictorial illusion: the scene is a freeze-frame. In Lionel Trilling's words, "The lovers exist only in the instant of their first sight of each other, without past or future, unhampered by that inner condition which we call personality."[9] The mate Leo has found waiting under the lamp post is portrayed as a prostitute, and in his eagerness and abundantly romantic imagination he may be rushing for his damnation. But even though Leo may be deluding himself, a more plausible reading is that he is moving toward an increasing honesty.[10] He has come to say, in the process of his search for a bride: "I came to God not because I loved Him, but because I did not" (p. 204). Passion has replaced Leo's former hesitant and prideful aloofness. By having Leo rush as he does to what even he knows will be the pain of his future, Malamud poises Leo between redemption and destruction. Stella might be the Jewish version of a Ligeia, but she more likely will make Leo a wife with whom he, as well as she, could discard their separate and false roles from the past. The static, pictorial image brings the story to a close, but the action and future developments remain undefined. Comparison with "Miriam" and "Where Are You Going, Where Have You Been?" reveals that the difference is thematic rather than structural and is not merely a matter of a hope as opposed to doom: Capote and Oates firmly predict disaster; Malamud implies rather than predicts fulfillment. By suspending the reader in the middle of an action Malamud gives the reader the sense of futurity, and in this way the story seems to extend horizontally beyond the endpoint.

Faulkner, "That Evening Sun"

Faulkner's "That Evening Sun" (1931), a story published previous to those we have just examined, is the most complex example of the special demands put on the reader by an open ending. Its truncated ending, even more abrupt than that of

"The Magic Barrel," is not the only such case in American literature—Frank Stockton's "The Lady or the Tiger" (1882) was a celebrated but largely isolated example. Nearer to his own time, Faulkner had Hemingway's "The Killers" as a model; Nancy sits in her cabin waiting for Jesus to attack much as Ole Andreson waits for his visitors.[11]

"That Evening Sun" differs significantly from many other stories that seem to suspend action. In John Cheever's "Chaste Clarissa" (1952), the success of the protagonist Baxter's seduction of Clarissa seems to lie beyond the end of the story, but there is no reasonable doubt: Baxter will succeed. He has managed to get Clarissa, an insecure young wife separated from her husband and left on an island with her mother-in-law, to air her opinions, and ludicrous, pathetic opinions they are. Baxter has seen "her face suffused with color and her pupils dilated" and "knew" that "the poor girl was lost." The final line encapsulates the story: "It was as simple as that."[12] The "it" can refer only to his success. The ending is resonant; for the reader "simple" triggers both comic and tragic reactions and stimulates imagining of further reverberations for Clarissa, who has been frank and ready to confess anything to her husband in the past. The ending can be omitted because the track of completion is so precisely laid down.

Hemingway's "The Killers" does not resolve whether Ole ever leaves his room. Here doubt is somewhat more probable: Al and Max are easily outsmarted in their first attempt to kill Ole. But Ole has accepted his fate, which seems inevitable. Furthermore, Hemingway has encapsulated Ole's story in order to shift the focus to its effect on Nick: "I'm going to get out of this town," Nick says, and that is the resolution of the story.[13] Ole will not leave, but Nick will.

Chekhov's "Lady with a Pet Dog," to choose an example outside of American literature, poses a different problem. The end of this story is appropriately the beginning of another: "And it seemed as though in a little while the solution would be

found, and then a new and glorious life would begin; and it
was clear to both of them that the end was still far off, and that
what was to be most complicated and difficult for them was
only just beginning."[14] The final word of the story, "beginning," seems appropriate to its openness. We cannot be certain
that Gurov has been transformed by his love of Anna; we
cannot be sure that "a new and glorious life would begin"—we
know that Gurov has seen a vision in the mirror, not of a new
life but of his own graying. But unlike "That Evening Sun,"
characters recognize the ironies of their position and are intent
on going forward; no definable action, a seduction or a
murder, hangs suspended, unfulfilled, awaiting the reader's
completion. The reader is encouraged to look out beyond the
moment of the ending with whatever mixture of emotions the
story has evoked but is not, so to speak, waiting for the other
shoe to drop. The characters themselves are aware of doubts
and hesitations, and the reader has been encouraged to share
and sympathize with their position.

Faulkner's strategy, unlike the methods of Cheever, Hemingway, and Chekhov, increases the uncertainty of the ending
while at the same time suspending the final action—Nancy's
anticipated death at the hands of her husband Jesus. The initial
narrative strategy, for instance, is indirect. After opening logically and coherently with observations about Monday washing rituals, which seems to predict a contrast between the
mechanized present and a slower, more genteel past, the narrator, Quentin, drifts from the discussion of all the Negro
washerwomen to a particular one, Nancy, who could walk
down a lane to a ditch near her house carrying a bundle on her
head that never wobbled or wavered. She could crawl on her
hands and knees through a fence, "her head rigid, uptilted, the
bundle steady as a rock or a balloon, and rise to her feet again
and go on," an image that implies repetition instead of requir-
ing resolution and seems to mark a story in the indirect
mode.[15] Quentin passes to a memory of how Nancy worked

for his family when Dilsey was sick and how the Compson children had to go to her house to wake her. They attributed her slowness in getting up to her drinking; later they learn of Nancy's attempt to hang herself and hear of her taking drugs. An image, the size of her stomach during the hanging attempt, leads to a conversation Quentin, Jason, and Candace overheard between Jesus and Nancy.

This discussion involves pure and not very accurate association—the assertion that Nancy was on cocaine was made by a jailer and does not seem likely, granted what seems to be more firsthand and therefore more reliable evidence in the rest of the story. Even the narrative voice is given to changing. Early in the story the narrator comments, with formal diction: "When Dilsey was sick in her cabin and Nancy was cooking for us, we could see her apron swelling out; that was before father told Jesus to stay away from the house"; after a passage of dialogue, without any other marker, the narrator changes to sentences with minimal embedding, repeating the same information: "Dilsey was still sick in her cabin. Father told Jesus to stay off our place. Dilsey was still sick. It was a long time. We were in the library after supper" (p. 292). Sentences have suddenly become a third of their former length; we seem to be in the mind of a child recalling verbatim his memories of the time, and that method continues for the rest of the story.

At this point the story suddenly diverts to the direct mode. Nancy has a problem—to avoid a confrontation with her husband Jesus, who has reputedly returned and waits to punish her (the father of the child she will bear is a white man), and she works out her problem by a series of linear steps. She is at first satisfied to be escorted home by Mr. Compson—"If I can just get through the lane . . . I be all right then" (p. 294)—but Mrs. Compson objects to being left alone. Nancy is granted a pallet in the kitchen, but that solution does not overcome her fears, and she utters what Quentin Compson can call only "the sound," after which her pallet is moved to the children's room.

The next day neither Mrs. Compson nor Dilsey wants to grant
her the privilege of staying with the children again. So Nancy
tries, and succeeds, in getting the Compson children to stay
with her.

The directness of the pattern is somewhat obscured by a
subplot. The central plot line is echoed and amplified by
Jason's fear of the same ditch in which Nancy fears Jesus is
hiding. Jason was frightened at that spot the previous Halloween; Candace intermittently taunts him about his fears, in
effect creating a story running parallel to Nancy's. Jason even
echoes the thematic core of the story, the issue of being
nothing but a "nigger," a word he bandies about with childish
insistence and arrogance. But instead of merely blending into
or supporting the main story, the subplot artfully plays against
it, interrupting it bizarrely, as if the narrator were working
back and forth between two radio stations whose messages
ironically serve as comments on each other.

Reading the story in the light of conventional narrative signals, we sense, as the action slows down and Nancy grows
frantic—as she goes to any length, even salvaging popcorn
kernels from the fire, to get the Compson children to stay—
that the climax approaches. To amuse the children, Nancy
begins to tell a story that only thinly disguises her own fears.
Candace interrupts, believing that she hears someone approaching. Nancy's terrified waiting is not unlike that of
Roderick Usher and the narrator in "The Fall of the House of
Usher" hearing footsteps in the hall during the reading of the
Mad Trist. Roderick, of course, is both rewarded and punished
by the deadly embrace he most fears and most wants, that of
his sister Madeline. Nancy's visitor is not Jesus but Mr. Compson, who takes the children home, leaving Nancy "sitting before
the fire" (p. 308).

Two ways of reading the story are established. The story
works toward an endpoint in an exaggeratedly traditional way,
but an endpoint that will not be provided. At the same time,

the vagrant sense of storytelling created by the indirect beginning may still affect the reader, diminishing the expectation of
an ending. The reader may be too uncertain about the state
of mind of the teller and the focus of the tale to identify a line
of action that could reasonably culminate in an ending—and
when the story does begin to assume its more conventional
pattern in the form of Nancy's fears, those parts that seem to
delay the ending, and that might under normal circumstances
merely be read as signals of the approaching end, are now
foregrounded as signals of a very different sort, signals that the
story will not come to closure. Put in the terms of the first half
of this study, the story begins in an apparently indirect manner,
that is, the narrator seems to delight in not identifying or
reaching a particular end. (The story is an extreme case of this
mode, for as I have used the term in the first half of the study, it
designates a story identifying the end, getting much of its
effect by clearly not going toward it; here no such end is
established.) Nancy's part of the story is direct. Any story in
direct mode has aspects of indirection subsumed within it—
the closer one gets to the end, the more the work slows down,
taking on the attributes of indirection. But if a direct tale is
embedded within an indirect one, this momentary appearance
of indirection of the direct mode can be read as a reassertion of
the original indirect mode. Figure and ground begin to exchange roles, and the anticipation of ending becomes ambiguous.

Whether the reader will settle for ambiguity is another matter. Some readers seem willing to: Cleanth Brooks has argued
that "we are not required to try to trace a portion of a picture
on out beyond the picture frame," but for Olga Vickery incompleteness encourages extension: "Faulkner's refusal to dra-
matize the conclusive action serves both to intensify the
dominant emotion and to project it beyond the story itself. By
this last Faulkner makes the reader implicitly accept the possibility of future continuation of the narrative and recognize

that his characters' lives extend beyond the formal confines of individual works."[16]

If we are willing to grant an extension, the next question is how we extend. Some readers consider Nancy's fears self-created. Olga Vickery claims that "a careful reading discovers how much emphasis is placed on the foolishness of her fears," and Jim Lee argues that Nancy's fear is imagined: "Read as the story of a woman dodging a vengeful husband, 'That Evening Sun' is a hide-and-seek thriller which cheats the reader by giving him no hint of the outcome. Read as the moral and mental disintegration of a woman who has sinned and is damned by her own guilt, it evokes the tragic emotions of pity and terror."[17]

It is not difficult to read the text this way. Nancy does not want something to happen; she wants something *not* to happen. She does not want an end, especially not an end to herself: "I aint going to see him again but once more, with that razor in his mouth" (p. 295). Retardations of action become not so much signals of an approaching climax as correlatives of Nancy's own internal state: facing what she regards as an inevitable end, she chooses to prolong the moment of its arrival as long as possible. The last thing Nancy wants is closure because the ambassador of closure has a razor in his mouth.

The possibility that Nancy's expectation of an end may be entirely self-created further contributes to the sense of openness. At first, Nancy does not name what she fears—the Compson children identify Jesus as the source of her fear. The more she talks of him, the more she fears that he waits for her. This fear is particularly evident at the end. Mr. Compson has asserted, "There's not a soul in sight," but Nancy insists, "He waiting in the ditch" (p. 307). Mr. Compson asks how she knows, and she explains that she has had a sign. She adds, "When yawl walk out that door, I gone." Mr. Compson calls that idea nonsense, and she then claims, "He looking through that window this minute, waiting for yawl to go. Then I gone." The more she fears, the more her fears become objective, leading to a spiral that must eventually end in anticlimax, for she cannot ultimately create the presence of her husband.

The prevailing critical sentiment, however, prefers a more ominous conclusion: the pressure of Nancy's expectation is so strong that it must be fulfilled, and the uninterested Compsons are powerless to prevent it. In John Hagopian's words, "It would be foolish to wonder if Nancy will actually be killed; of course she will—all the lines of force in the story move powerfully in that direction."[18]

Norms that one might customarily use to choose between these two interpretations are not available. Should we trust the father (the elder Jason Compson) and assume he is right that Nancy should be left in the cabin? Cleanth Brooks claims that "it would be difficult—if not impossible—for anyone to free Nancy from her terror and that most men would have acted pretty much as Mr. Compson did," but May Brown accuses him of being "clearly callous" in his assumed gallantry and insensitive for suggesting that Jesus has taken another wife in St. Louis.[19] Although we may attribute the difference to the sex of each critic, it is more reasonable to assume that the dispute further illustrates James's dictum about the interrelation of character and plot. Without closure to complete the plot—unless we know whether he was right—we cannot know whether the elder Jason Compson was reasonable.

Some readings are essentially attempts to provide closure by finding a new figure—a closed figure—in the carpet. One critic has argued that Caddy is central to the story, and she dominates the final moment: "It is this voice that Quentin hears now even as he perceives, in remembering, how right Caddy had been, how Faulkner's heart's darling at seven had known all along how the characters of 'That Evening Sun' would turn out," namely, that they are all, in Caddy's words, "scairy cats."[20] The virtue of this reading is that it explains why the story ends on what would otherwise seem an extraneous squabble between the children, and it is unquestionably true that Caddy insistently probes to have adults explicitly verbalize the significance of each incident. But it is not plausible to assume that Quentin tells the story because he realizes Caddy had understood better than anyone else. His own understanding at least of the facts is implicitly in advance of that of the other children, and explicitly twice: Caddy is willing to go with Nancy not because of any real sympathy with Nancy's position (later she will support Jason in an effort to leave when the popcorn making fails) but because she wants to define her boldness in distinction to Jason's fear: "'I'm not afraid to go,' Caddy said. 'Jason is the one that's afraid.'" Caddy rationalizes, arguing that Mother has not forbidden them to go: "She didn't say we couldn't," but Quentin calls her on that: "'We didn't ask,' I said" (p. 300). Since Quentin's understanding was in advance at the time, it is unlikely that he has changed his mind in the retelling. John Hagopian's characterization of Caddy as "a lively, inquisitive pest" seems more accurate.[21]

Individual lines such as Quentin's question about "who will do our washing now" (p. 309) have also received undue emphasis as determiners of Nancy's fate. Pearson commented that "the apparently unfeeling query is Quentin's recognition of the finality of Nancy's fate. It is his way of acknowledging, even by the faintest terms of involvement, his initiation into an adult knowledge of evil which neither Caddy nor Jason shares."[22]

Quentin's question indicates that he believes at this point that Nancy will die but does not serve to prove that she did. We need again to look at the consistency of Quentin's position. In the opening paragraph he indulges himself in a reverie about the past and present, concluding that the present is unsatisfactory, visualizing parts of telephone poles as "bloated and ghostly and bloodless grapes" and cars fleeing "apparitionlike behind alert and irritable electric horns," in contrast to the stately vision of the past when "Negro women with, balanced on their steady, turbaned heads, bundles of clothes tied up in sheets, almost as large as cotton bales, carried so without touch of hand between the kitchen door of the white house and the blackened washpot beside a cabin door in Negro Hollow" (p. 289). Quentin understood facts even as a child but as an adult, still does not understand meanings. He did not understand the guilt of white use of the Negro as a child and does not understand fifteen years later when he tells the story, nostalgic for a past the reader sees riddled with corruption. Quentin's question about who will do the washing at the end is not just apparently unfeeling—it *is* unfeeling and simply that, not an acknowledgment of complicity in evil. In the same way, the father's lack of response to Quentin's question may tell the reader that he too thinks more about Nancy's uses than her safety, but it tells little more. Father does not respond because a quarrel again erupts between Jason and Caddy, and that absorbs his attention. To assume that the father knows Nancy is as good as dead on the basis of his distraction is an unreasonable attempt to turn around the consistency of his effort and assertion throughout the rest of the work.

The need of most readers to supply an ending is so strong that it has led such a critic as Malcolm Cowley to assume that a passage from *The Sound and the Fury* reveals that Nancy was murdered and left in the ditch for vultures. Stephen Whicher refutes this claim, demonstrating that the reference is probably to a horse, and comments, "Not even in Faulkner's South are murdered Negroes left in a ditch, in the sight of children, for vultures to eat."[23]

To what extent is it possible to resolve the issue? There are, after all, closural signals. The children are leaving Nancy and Nancy's sounds recede, both in a sense encapsulating the image, and the leaving is the opposite of the first mention of her, the image of the Compson children chunking rocks at her door to get her up in the morning. The image of Nancy has developed over a curve of action, from the washerwoman with a "balanced bundle and the hat that never bobbed or wavered," to a woman who cannot hold a cup of coffee in her hands, to a tired woman sitting in the cabin with the door open. Imagery patterns have a completed antithetical balance; the coldness of the opening image, Nancy by a cold stove, is inverted in the heat and fumes of the cabin and Nancy burning her hands on the lamp. Nancy's terror has its climax in the tears that run down her face, "each one a little turning ball of firelight" (p. 306). Her comment following father's arrival, after which she subsides into acceptance of her fate—"I reckon what I going to get aint no more than mine"—is the opposite of her reiterated complaint that "it aint no fault of mine." The restless movement of her hands has subsided: "She talked quieter now, and her face looked quiet, like her hands" (p. 308).

If we can ignore for a moment certain difficulties with the final paragraphs and certain structural problems, we can see that within "That Evening Sun" rests an essentially complete story, that of Nancy's undoing for reasons real or imagined. Her situation is parallel to Laura's in "Flowering Judas": Laura's unconscious speaks to her in a dream, and she is left wide awake, afraid to go back to sleep, just as Nancy cannot sleep. The title, "That Evening Sun," echoes the "St. Louis Blues"—the ironies are marked: the lover in the "St. Louis Blues" has the urge when the sun goes down to flee and join the man who has left her, in contrast to Nancy, fixed, unable to flee, and the cause of her man's leaving—but the echo also reaches back both to Ephesians of the New Testament and Amos of the Old.

These associations ground the story as firmly within a biblical tradition as the inverted mass at the end of "Flowering Judas" and provide a sense of completion by drawing out the moral significance. In Ephesians, readers of the letter (who, unlike Nancy, are characterized as about to arise from the dead) are urged to observe social rules: wives are to be subject to their husbands, children to their parents, slaves to their earthly masters. Faulkner's story is Ephesians upside down. Nancy has fallen into prostitution, Jason is holding out for chocolate cake, and Jesus has been ordered away from the Compson household. The ironically named Jesus of this story is not following scripture: "Be angry but do not sin; do not let the sun go down on your anger" (Ephesians 4:26). The vision of the story is much closer to Amos, in which the Lord threatens to make the "sun go down at noon" (Amos 8:9). Nancy has fulfilled the terms of the prophecy, "Your wife shall be a harlot in the city" (7:17) and the rich "trample the head of the poor into the dust of the earth" (2:7)—Stovall has knocked down Nancy and kicked her in the mouth with his heel. Seen in this context, "That Evening Sun" is a complete depiction of social and psychological ruin, a reading that is further clarified when one sets the story in the context of the last of the village section of *The Collected Stories*, a section which, as Philip Momberger has argued, reveals a total destruction of the sense of village, the sense of community.[24]

As complete as this version might be, we must still take into account the suspension created by the structure and the final paragraphs. Faulkner obscures, even contradicts, the sense of finality created by many elements of the story. He has constantly shifted the reader's expectation by alternating the direct and indirect methods, and he has given strong indications that Nancy is building her own fears. He has opened up the final passages—Nancy returns to her previous abjuration of responsibility ("It aint no fault of mine"), the "sound" commences again—and then he ends on the discordance of the children's squabble, its comic tonality remote from the anger and rebellion that Jesus' intentions supposedly represent. And above all the action is incomplete, making us wonder whether we are to assume that Nancy dies or does not die, or whether we are meant to hold the end in suspended judgment.

Faulkner's own brief comment on the story may help. It

would seem at first that he has not wished to deal with the problem of the openness of the ending; all he has said is that Nancy "knew that when the crisis of her need came, the white family wouldn't be there."[25] The phrase "her need" is suitably ambiguous, for it could refer either to the real need for protection or for a psychological need to deal with her guilt in the consequences of her act. Leaving off the ending clarifies the story in Faulkner's own terms of need and failure to be there, for we can see the price she is going to pay and how far she or the Compsons are from seeing the irony that if Jesus *is* taking vengeance on her, he is misguided, for he could rightly do what he had actually threatened, take vengeance against the white community.

A comment of Nancy's to Mr. Compson about his seeing her at work the next day could serve to identify the reader's final position: "You'll see what you'll see, I reckon. . . . But it will take the Lord to say what that will be" (p. 308). Faulkner has, I suggest, purposely deprived us of knowledge and does not want us to complete the action, as his various narrative strategies demonstrate. The result, in Faulknerian language, is a "furious tableau," a stationary scene as pictorial as the end of "Flowering Judas" and "The Magic Barrel." The scene is filled with the reader's need to extend it (to draw inferences beyond the picture's frame) but suspended by balances of closure and anticlosure (and thus held within the frame).

This suspension may serve several purposes. Just as the viewpoint of the children and the young Quentin forces us into the story, makes the reader feel he is discovering more than they can, so too the suspension puts the reader in Nancy's position, makes the reader submit, if not to terror, at least to an unnerving irresolution. It also engages us on the intellectual level, making us question whether it matters if Jesus is there or not. This is a portrait of a woman undone; this is pure fear. And finally, the suspension may force the reader to consider the circumstances and significance of that terror. Faulkner may not expect the reader, as Cheever does in "Chaste Clarissa," to know exactly how to complete the story. Rather, he might be turning the energy that we put into closing a story back into the story and investing this receding picture, the Compsons leaving Nancy behind, with its full experiential weight and significance. We need to see that the terror, although partly self-created, is logical and virtually necessary, and we need to see that ironically Nancy bears the cost of broken social relationships while the rest of the community, white and black, sees no complicity, sees no connection between use and degradation. Who will do our washing? Quentin asks, and his question in this light regains its full irony, revealing the shortsightedness fundamental to the whole social problem.

Faulkner's effort to untell his story as much as to tell it is an index of how much short-story form has altered since Poe's characterization of the genre. Although no story is ever wholly enclosed and self-consuming—in "The Fall of the House of Usher," for instance, the gaps and Usher's accusation that the narrator is mad encourage the reader to comprehend more extensively than the narrator, and in that way the story slips beyond its temporal frame and out of perfect enclosure— Poe's sense of story, typified in "The Fall of the House of Usher," nevertheless depends primarily on convergence of closural signals. Faulkner, nearly a hundred years later, could tell his terror story and mix the resolved and unresolved elements in the structure, trusting the reader to make the right choices in assembling the meaning and, one might assume, full well knowing how much he asked the reader to do. In 1931 this fractured structure was atypical, but thirty years later, with the advent of the subject of the next chapter, the antistory, disorienting the reader was no longer such an obscure and uncommon objective.

CHAPTER 7

Antistory and
Story: From Tralfamadore
to Tale

The Semblance of Narrative

In Kurt Vonnegut's *Slaughterhouse-Five*, Billy Pilgrim, bored with the only book in English left for him on his trip to Tralfamadore (the book happens to be *The Valley of the Dolls*), asks for a Tralfamadorian novel. The one he is given, containing "clumps of symbols separated by stars," he cannot read. He guesses that the clumps are telegrams; his Tralfamadorian host tells him that his surmise is in some ways wrong but also in certain respects correct:

> Each clump of symbols is a brief, urgent message—describing a situation, a scene. We Tralfamadorians read them all at once, not one after the other. There isn't any particular relationship between all the messages, except that the author has chosen them carefully, so that, when seen all at once, they produce an image of life that is beautiful and surprising and deep. There is no beginning, no middle, no end, no suspense, no moral, no causes, no effects. What we love in our books are the depths of many marvelous moments seen all at one time.[1]

Although Vonnegut is not defining the short story in this passage, the quotation does serve as an emblem of the basic impulse that generated compressed form and imagist form—the impulse to forsake narrative, its linear movement, causality,

144

suspense, and end-direction, in favor of a single, complex image or a series of images without causal relations. Such an image would supposedly reflect the truth of experience, thus affecting the reader directly, leading him to the total grasp of the story that Poe envisaged. Poe argued that the tale, unlike the novel, could be comprehended at a single sitting, during which time "the soul of the reader is at the writer's control."[2] This Tralfamadorian desire cannot be fully achieved in either the short story or the novel, both of which are condemned to be read linearly, but it serves as a goal toward which writers could strive. Even a writer who most frequently works along traditional lines, Joyce Carol Oates, has longed to tell a story "as if it were sheer lyric, all its components present simultaneously."[3] Writers of what has come to be known as the anti-story are the closest to embodying Tralfamadorian ideals, and in their striving to impose this design we can see new uses for old, end-directed narrative expectations and new applications for old methods of securing closure.

Examined in light of the Tralfamadorian elements, antistories can be divided into two kinds, those that begin as standard narrative but into which reflexive awareness of Tralfamadorian elements slowly penetrates, altering the narrative flow, or those that make no pretense of narrative organization and instead present themselves as a collection of parts. This second type, more purely Tralfamadorian, is more significant in the context of this study, but the first, illustrated by Robert Coover's "The Babysitter" (1971), is more common (Donald Barthelme uses it frequently in stories such as "Glass Mountain" and "The Indian Uprising"), and it shows how narrative and nonnarrative elements might interact.

Coover, "The Babysitter"

"The Babysitter" starts with a common situation, parents going out for the evening, a bit rushed, leaving the children with a babysitter, and at first the minor dislocations and discomforts advance the story as if it were a simple exercise in the direct pattern. The story has a built-in termination: the Tuckers' leaving their children with a babysitter while they enjoy an evening out predicts their return. Typographically the story resembles a Tralfamadorian novel; it is a series of sections, 106 in all, separated by dots.

Through the first half dozen paragraphs the dots seem to mark only the breaks between changing points of view—an objective presentation from the kitchen, Mr. Tucker upstairs, the expectations of Jack (a boy who knows the babysitter will spend the evening at the Tucker house), what the babysitter sees as she enters the house. We assume that the events are sometimes simultaneous, sometimes in chronological order. The exact time relations do not seem significant because there appears to be a common theme, the expectation of the Tuckers' leaving.

Soon, however, internal contradictions arise. The babysitter gives the Tucker children a bath, or she herself takes a bath. The reader might at first restore the harmony of the accounts by assuming these are separate events, both of which take place. The children take a bath *and* the sitter takes a bath. But the possibilities that center around the bathtub eventually multiply too rapidly to be encompassed by this thesis. Jack and his friend Mark arrive and join the babysitter in the tub, or perhaps they never arrive at all and might still be playing pinball, or perhaps Mr. Tucker was the one who arrived, leaving his wife lying on the floor at a party, her girdle around her ankles, with their host for the evening standing above her, inexplicably smeared with butter. If Jack is in the tub, did he succeed in his designs on the babysitter, or did she keep him at bay? If Mr. Tucker was in the tub, did he have more luck with her than Jack, or did he fall and whack his head on the sink? This is Tralfamadore gone berserk, for these moments do not merely coexist, and they hardly coalesce to form a beautiful image of life.

In such an unusual situation the ending will play an especially significant role. The ending might possibly unravel all the various strands and explain them all, sorting out the various lines, selecting one and explaining the falseness of the others. Coover does not provide such an ending. The reader must rely on evidence of natural termination. True to the pattern of the work to this point, Coover provides several conflicting natural terminations. First is a death terminator: possibly the sitter, in her haste to take care of one of the children, Jimmy, and in her haste to answer the phone (the caller may be either Jack or Mr. Tucker), leaves the baby unattended in the tub, and as Jimmy announces, something may be wrong with the baby: "It's down in the water and it's not swimming or anything."[4] Possibly the sitter is the one who has succumbed. In another section, one of the boys stands over the inert sitter and says, "You just tilted her, man!" (p. 237).

Another terminator is the summary—the collection of all the characters in a final tableau, with Mrs. Tucker, her ripped girdle around her ankles, asking, "What are the four of you doing in the bathtub with *my* babysitter?" If this were the true ending, all the fantasies and humiliations would coexist.

That section is not the terminal paragraph. In a subsequent paragraph Coover terminates more placidly—the dishes are done, the children in bed, and the babysitter dozes. In the section after that the Tuckers rush home, thinking they have heard something about a babysitter on TV. The next section seems to deny that possibility: the babysitter "wakes, startled, to find Mr. Tucker hovering over her. 'I must have dozed off!' she exclaims. 'Did you hear the news about the babysitter?' Mr. Tucker asks. 'Part of it,' she says, rising. 'Too bad, wasn't it?' Mr. Tucker is watching the report of the ball scores and golf tournaments. 'I'll drive you home in just a minute, dear,' he says. 'Why how nice!' Mrs. Tucker exclaims from the kitchen. 'The dishes are all done!'"[5] This passage seems to link to the section four paragraphs earlier, reestablishing the stability of the opening paragraph, the tension of which is now brought to rest. But there is one more paragraph: "'What can I say, Dolly?'" the host says with a sigh, twisting the buttered strands of her ripped girdle between his fingers. 'Your children are murdered, your husband gone, a corpse in your bathtub, and your house is wrecked. I'm sorry. But what can I say?' On the TV, the news is over, and they're selling aspirin. 'Hell, I don't know,' she says. 'Let's see what's on the late late movie'" (p. 239). There is ultimately no single ending to this hydra of stories. The real ending is all of the endings, the opposition between complete tranquillity and complete destruction. It ends by a virtual catalog of the devices available at the antithesis level because no problem level, in the ordinary sense, remains. The ending is an abstract, tonal performance, an array of possible endings held in suspension by opposition.

The Rejection of Narrative

Barthelme, "Balloon," and Gass, "In the Heart of the Heart of the Country"

Stories of the second kind, those that do not pretend to conventional narrative form, are less common. They usually masquerade as something like an essay because the word "story" does not seem to apply. Many of Barthelme's stories fit into this category. "On Angels" *(City Life)*, an example of the essay form, centers on what angels will do now that God is dead; "At the Tolstoy Museum" *(City Life)* proceeds as if it were an essay in art criticism. Occasionally the grafting of one genre upon another can lead to interesting results and to unusual terminations. "The Balloon" (1966), for instance, seems to be largely about an image of a huge balloon hanging over the space from Fourteenth Street to Central Park: "There were no situations, simply the balloon hanging there," the narrator maintains, an idea without narrative movement, something close to a pure image unembedded in a story.[6] The balloon is described, we learn of various uses to which the balloon is put, and then interpretations of the balloon are offered, and it is seen as a symbol or an art object. Though this pattern of development is without overt linear direction, it is not without tension, for all the hypotheses make it progressively more difficult to imagine the balloon as a physical object, while increasing the reader's need to account for and understand it. The longer the piece continues, the more we are encouraged to read it as a narrative, to search for causal relations. The final paragraph in particular ends as if the account of the balloon had been a narrative after all:

> I met you under the balloon, on the occasion of your return from Norway; you asked if it was mine; I said it was. The balloon, I said, is a spontaneous autobiographical disclosure, having to do with the unease I felt at your absence, and with sexual deprivation, but now that your visit to Bergen has been terminated, it is no longer necessary or appropriate. Removal of the balloon was easy; trailer trucks carried away the depleted fabric, which is now stored in West Virginia, awaiting some other time of unhappiness, sometime, perhaps, when we are angry with one another. [P. 22.]

The ending mixes the closed and the open, closed in the sense that the balloon is deflated, packed up, and that an explanation for its appearance has been offered, one that has led to its disappearance. This explanation has an operative efficiency that the other hypotheses lack. But the snap of the final sentences, the threat of the balloon being brought out again some other time, momentarily opens the story. The revelation that the balloon represents a domestic spat also works against closure. The previous paragraph had put the balloon to grand metaphysical uses, but of all the explanations offered, the last one is the most tenuous, the one that least accounts for the size and mysteriousness of the object. It is an overly tidy ending to a mounting complexity and as such should leave a residue of dissatisfaction, which, of course, within the framework of the story, is just the opposite, that is, satisfaction in the realization that the balloon cannot really be tidied up, moralized, and packed away.

I cannot argue that all stories of this type can be reconstructed by narrative interpretation. William Gass's "In the Heart of the Heart of the Country" (1967), which comes close to the Tralfamadorian goal, is particularly intransigent to traditional narrative analysis. The story is divided into thirty-two sections with titles such as "weather," "politics," "vital data," "education," "business," as if they were parts of a chamber of commerce report. The section headings appear on the average of three times each but without patterned distribution or discernible development within sections under the same heading.

Most readers, I believe, will nevertheless try to impose narrative assumptions on the story. The compressed form, for instance, encourages the reader to construct a narrative on the basis of very tenuous clues, and those expectations now affect our reading of all contemporary fiction. The procedure for reading compressed stories requires us to regard all clues about motion in space as crucial indicators and to see any repetitions, however slight, as signs of central concern. Any statement can predict an outcome. When we find the narrator declaring he is "in retirement from love," we assume the story will lead to the opposite, the restoration of love, or the final demonstration, after movement to the contrary, that the retirement is in fact final.[7] One passage, in which the narrator refers to an apparent lover from the past, has a number of closural features: "I am not here; I've passed the glass, passed second-story spaces, flown by branches, brilliant berries, to the ground, grass high in seed and leafage every season; and it is the same as when I passed above you in my aged, ardent body; it's in short, a kind of love; and I am learning to restore myself, my house, my body, by paying court to gardens, cats, and running water, and with neighbors keeping company" (p. 183). Were this passage placed at the end, it would rightly be perceived as terminal, for the excitement, the sense of affirmation, the claims of identity of major thematic elements, the summary catalog, and the way it resolves the "retirement from love" issue would indicate that the story has come to a close. But this passage comes one-third of the way into the work, and the remaining two-thirds undo all of it. The pastoral retreat of the landscape becomes "a lie of old poetry"; "nature in the old sense . . . does not exist" (p. 194). The character identified as "you" is never particularized; instead of gaining identity, the figure is dispersed into other personalities: "Sometimes you're Tom Sawyer, Huckleberry Finn; it is perpetually summer; your buttocks are my pillow; we are adrift on a raft; your back is our river. . . . Sometimes you are soft like a shower of water; you are bread in my mouth" (p. 188).

Closural signals at the actual end are minimal. In the final section the narrator listens to an audio speaker at Christmas time playing "Joy to the World," but even these signals are partially canceled: "There's no one to hear the music but myself, and though I'm listening, I'm no longer certain. Perhaps the record's playing something else" (p. 206). Allusions to Yeats's "Sailing to Byzantium" also imply an obscure circularity—the story opened with the line "So I have sailed the seas and come" (p. 172) and closes with references to towers, boughs, and metallic strains, all echoes of Yeats's poem—but this is closure by association, not a close to a plot.

Narrative in this story is not fractured for pleasure, to demonstrate the author's dexterity, as sometimes seems the case in stories by Barth, Barthelme, or Coover. Instead, the consistent frustration of narrative expectations highlights the intransigence of the story, effectively correlating the narrator's state of mind. A midwesterner who listens to the story of his fellow villagers much as George Willard did in *Winesburg, Ohio*, this narrator is no youth free to escape, as did Willard, and the

resistance of the text to narrative organization is a precise
equivalent for the narrator's experience. As in "That Evening
Sun" the reader experiences the limits of his desire to apply
closure, to create form. The conventions we apply as readers
are not meant to smooth over inconsistencies, to refashion the
story into the lines of something we already know. We must
surrender our conventions, and we must confront the story on
its own terms. Our inability to anticipate or apply closure puts
us in the heart of the heart of a world, and we must give over to
the strangeness in which we find ourselves.

I do not mean to suggest by the organization of this section
that the rejection of narrative, as a consequence of the reaching
toward simultaneity, toward openness and freedom from
pointing toward the end, is the goal toward which narrative is
evolving; narrative from the time of Chaucer has always had
an indirect tradition, one that rejects the primacy of the ending
either as a structural device or as a way of looking at the world.
Strong as the Tralfamadorian urge is, and it is one that seems
particularly adaptable to the brevity of the short story, the need
for linearity, for narrative, will nearly always emerge as long as
stories are told in strings of words. We can see the strength of
this narrative urge by looking in some detail at John Cheever's
"Artemis, the Honest Well Digger," for Cheever's storytelling
is at once a mixture of some of the oldest forms of tale telling
with the newest narrative and closural freedoms.

The Tale in Modern Perspective

Cheever, "Artemis, the Honest Well Digger"

In many respects Cheever shares the concerns of modern
short-story writers from Sherwood Anderson through
William Gass; he has avowed his distaste for fiction whose
form is clearly apparent, particularly fiction shaped by the
causal sequence of plot. "I don't work with plots," he has

claimed, "I work with intuition, apprehension, dreams, concepts." Access to the psychic depth cannot be provided by rational and orderly design: "A good narrative," he has fancifully proposed, "is a rudimentary structure, rather like a kidney."[8] Although some Cheever stories display conventional narrative structure—"The Enormous Radio" is a classic example of direct form—many illustrate the extent of his rejection of traditional plotting and demonstrate how closure can be achieved and can control the form of a story even when the writer, as have many since World War I, works away from rather than toward an ending.

Many of Cheever's stories of this type, and "Artemis, the Honest Well Digger" (1972) is a typical example, are clearly indirect to the point of resembling the antecedent of the modern short story, the tale. Even in the first paragraph, prospects for order, for a progression and a complete experience that will reveal a shape and design, do not seem promising. The topic of the paragraph is water, or more precisely Artemis's belief that water is all-important, a theme seemingly too abstract to be tested by succeeding events in a fictionally interesting way. What satisfaction is the reader likely to have if Artemis's belief is either proved or disproved? The significance of water seems to be the thesis of an essay, not a story. By concluding the paragraph with a series of definitions—"Man was largely water. Water was man. Water was love. Water was water," leaping from reversed identities to generalities, then terminating with a virtual identity—Cheever reduces the concept of water to a verbal echo.[9] The problem of the significance of water, weak as it is as a generator of further events, seems to have been reduced to meaninglessness before the story is even under way. And if, as readers accustomed to fiction in the traditional sense, we have lost confidence in the author for his handling of the first paragraph, we are not likely to be aroused by the second: "To get the facts out of the way" (p. 650), it begins, as if our narrator were all too aware of the traditional expository needs of narrative and bored with the duty of proceeding.

Cheever then takes us through Artemis's life chronologically, as the writer of a tale customarily does, showing us what made Artemis choose well-drilling over other professions, including technical writing. The focus of the remaining action (other than the significance of water) is not revealed until the scene with Artemis and a lusty, hard-drinking divorcee "whose backside seemed almost too good to be true" (p. 652). The first use of scene rather than summary further emphasizes the centrality of this new part of Artemis's life. A second scene, with Mrs. Filler, who has designs on Artemis, continues to establish the pattern. The pursuit of love as the focus of the story is confirmed when, three times within a few paragraphs, Artemis is described as wanting to escape these women so he can pursue a girl fresh as the one pictured on an oleomargarine package. This comic embodiment of a more conventional problem does promise a conclusion. Artemis is a sexual innocent despite his adventures, and the reader then attempts to estimate which direction his predicted education will take him, whether the purity of his desire is a reasonable goal, and whether he will find a girl who embodies his ideal.

Even with the problem established, the course of events continually diverges. Mrs. Filler has fallen in love with Artemis, has told him so, and has also reported her feelings to her absent, soon to return husband. Artemis sees "that the time to travel has arrived" (p. 658). He goes to a travel agent, who talks him into going to Russia. Upon arriving, he is informed that Khrushchev has decided to welcome him "as a member of the American proletariat" (p. 660). This direction is quickly abandoned, however, for Khrushchev is deposed before meeting Artemis, and Artemis falls in love with a tourist guide, Natasha Funaroff. Fresh and girlish even though mature, she approximates the ideal of the oleomargarine girl, a point which Cheever does not need to establish overtly.

THE TALE IN MODERN PERSPECTIVE

If Cheever has refocused our attention on the original theme by introducing Natasha, he is nevertheless in no hurry to conclude. He does not hesitate to develop any absurdity he fancies. He has already dallied earlier in the story with the irony that Mrs. Filler's husband has written a book called *Shit*, which has been translated into twelve languages and published in paperback. Had Artemis, Cheever asserts, been walking down a street in China instead of reading the book, he "would have felt no more alien than he felt at that moment, trying to comprehend the fact that he lived in a world where a man was wealthy and esteemed for having written a book about turds" (p. 654). The images Cheever can fashion from the idea of Filler's "lyrical descriptions of nature—loose bowels in a lemon grove in Spain, constipation in a mountain pass in Nepal, dysentery on the Greek Islands" (p. 655), seem infinitely expandable, limited and unified only by Artemis's slightly indignant astonishment. The energy of the story seems to squander itself in byways, here in the Filler episode and again with Natasha. Once Artemis's affair with Natasha is terminated by the Russian government, one of whose agents whisks away Artemis with the comment that there is no such person as Natasha, Cheever again elaborates what was in the beginning a logical progression, namely that Artemis and Natasha write letters, into an expansive episode in its own right, as if the narrator so loved the charm and irony of communication over such distance, the non sequiturs, the poetry, the pathetic irrationality of customs put into words, that he cannot control himself. "Tonight is Halloween," writes Artemis, "I don't suppose you have that in Russia. It is the night when the dead are supposed to arise, although they don't, of course, but children wander around the streets disguised as ghosts and skeletons and devils and you give them candies and pennies. Please come to my country and marry me" (p. 667). Natasha responds with correspondence equally poetic, with her image of their letters "flapping their wings at each other somewhere

over the Atlantic." Natasha's observations are as original as
Artemis's: "I always thought God sat on the clouds, surrounded by troops of angels, but perhaps He lives in a sub-
marine, surrounded by divisions of mermaids" (p. 667). The
letters reveal passion and loss, especially when Natasha writes
of seeing a splash of white on the bottom of her mailbox, left
by painters, and believes she has had a letter from him: "My
heart beats and I run to the box, only to find white paint"
(p. 668).

Insofar as closure is derived from culmination of the action
of the plot, the prospect of a close to this series of actions seems
distant and unlikely. But there are aspects of the story which
draw it back together against the centrifugal pull of a plot
whose moment-to-moment sequence is tangential. The two
themes, the importance of water and the search for the
oleomargarine girl, are on the surface separate but at the core
similar. Both are searches for purity, for perfection, for es-
sences that sustain and refresh. The similarity is underlined by
references to the opposite of purity: pollution—DDT in the
water, Mr. Filler's pollution of the world's bookshelves by a
topic that is pollution itself. And because of Artemis's obsession, even his lovemaking takes on overtones of the search for
water. When Mrs. Filler dips her head on him like a "bird
going after seed or water," he responds by saying, "Big load's
on its way, big load's coming down the line" (p. 657), creating
analogies between two quite different kinds of gushers. His
incurable fascination with words like "cacaphony," "percussion," and "throbbingly" seems to grow from his profession.
Ultimately even the phrase "water is love," meaningless at
first, takes on some sense in context. The creation of metaphoric links and analogies is a force for wholeness but a weak
determiner of closure.

Having advanced the continuing passion of the lovers during their exchange of letters, a motion that has a clear direction
and promises termination, whether fulfillment or loss,

Cheever again diverges. The American government calls in
Artemis for an investigation. Artemis makes his way from
office to office to determine what his government asks of him.
The climax of his search, and of the story, occurs in this paragraph, in which an American official from the State Department announces to Artemis that he knows Artemis has been
writing to Natasha:

> Of course, we've monitored your letters. Their government
> does the same. Our intelligence feels that your letters contain
> some sort of information. She, as the daughter of a marshal, is
> close to the Government. The rest of her family were shot. She
> wrote that God might sit in a submarine, surrounded by divi-
> sions of mermaids. That same day was the date of our last
> submarine crisis, I understand that she is an intelligent woman
> and I can't believe that she would write anything so foolish
> without its having a second meaning. Earlier she wrote that
> you and she were a wave on the Black Sea. The date corre-
> sponds precisely to the Black Sea maneuvers. You sent her a
> photograph of yourself beside the Wakusha Reservoir, point
> out that this was the center of the Northeast watershed. This,
> of course, is not classified information, but it all helps. Later
> you write that the dark seems to you like a house divided into
> seventy rooms. This was written ten days before we activated
> the Seventieth Division. Would you care to explain any of this?
> [P. 670.]

The passage contains a large number of terminal features. It
supplies the explanation of the most recent episode, the calling
of Artemis to Washington, and it ties together tightly within
one paragraph a review of what had been a dispersed series of
observations in several letters. And it purports to generalize,
to explain the significance of what otherwise would have been
a series of unrelated figurative observations. Under disorder is
revealed the suggestion of plan. Other strands may also come
together for the reader, for if earlier the Russians have exposed
their foolishness, their reliance on bureaucracy, their irrational

suppositions and acts, the same is now true of the Americans. These two poles of world power now stand parallel in their manipulation, in this case in a relatively harmless way, of the individual for state purposes. The only significance available is then presumably a private one, a relation of individual to individual, Artemis to Natasha, not the relation of man to his country.

The passage is, of course, in the common sense no conclusion at all. "Intelligence" is revealed as a sort of misguided literary criticism. The state officers' report fills in no gaps, ties no knots. And the passage has nothing to do with the theme, the quest for the oleomargarine girl. And yet the passage contributes to closure after all. It is the ultimate gesture of a narrator who all along has defied expectations. The air of finality resulting from review of disparate elements in tighter form, the leap to generalization, the suggestion of symmetry, all hold together as an ending whether what is actually being tied together, leaped to, and symmetried have any substance at all. This is the form of an ending, and it is form that counts.

After this point the tale winds down by diminution and encapsulation. Artemis never again hears from the State Department, the word "never" carrying the sense of finality. He writes four circumspect, nonpoetic letters and gets no reply. The spot of paint is mentioned, echoing an emotional high point of the story. The final paragraph concludes with the healing sound of rain, and healing is a reference to well-being, a movement toward natural termination. The final sentence is two words: "Water, water," a balanced repetition no more plausible than the initial equation of water to everything else and then to itself. We have returned to the water theme of the opening, but water has been tied to love in only the most tenuous way, so that whatever sense of satisfaction we might have must come from the idea of return itself, not from the significance of the return and its relation to the developing themes of the story. Again, form, not substance, provides closure.

As is typical of so many stories since "Hands," progress toward closural signals is neither uniform nor incremental. Design in the modern story may be teasingly present, then absent, and the design itself may even be foregrounded. The expectation and fulfillment of closure are detachable in many modern stories from what Poe called the singleness of effect, but they are no less operative as controllers of the reader's experience. The closed, single form that Poe advocated is the product of the initial discovery of form within the genre; once that pattern was established, subsequent writers have been free to use the anticipation of closural patterns in more varied ways. Narrative is extremely flexible, and although our requirements for the interactions of the various levels of closure have changed, the possibilities are so varied that we may trust forms will continue to evolve and proliferate, for each innovation serves as an additional element of the narrative grid the experienced reader brings to every story and thus serves to increase the range of possibilities for the writer. Our toleration for "unclosed" experience has greatly increased, with only minimal and often purely formal signals now sufficing to mark the wholeness and completeness of a story.

CHAPTER 8

Conclusion

My goal throughout this study has been to make readers more conscious of one aspect of reading: how the anticipation of completion in all of its various forms, in space, in time, and at the level of theme and idea, structures the story and the reader's experience of it.

The way in which closure has affected the history of the genre, I have argued, further demonstrates the validity of the theoretical model. When Poe realized, both in practice and theory, that the writer's anticipation of an ending could shape the rest of the story, he had perceived something only partly realized in the efforts of short-story writers before him. He had sensed the hypnotic effect that a short narrative, read in between ten minutes to an hour, might exert if latent with the sense of ultimate approach. The short story was long enough to sustain this mounting intensity, which only the imminence of a goal could create, but it was not so long that natural and social needs would invariably break the spell. He realized how the sense of goal could structure all of the work; he realized that the effort of memory required to match the beginning and end, at least at a subconscious level, was within the reader's range.

The short story is that genre in which anticipation of the ending is always present. Irving, Twain, Jewett, and Cheever seem to work otherwise, but their efforts only prove the point. The form can be put to advantage against its central tendency, and in fact this contrary use of expectation often seems more creative and exciting than formal fulfillment of the genre's properties. An argument for the diversity of the short story— Ian Reid, for one, rejects the centrality of Poe's Hawthorne review—demonstrates the richness and variety of the genre, but diversity should not obscure the genre's fundamental dependence on an endpoint, whether the story works toward it or teasingly avoids it.[1] For all its diversity, the short story is a surprisingly coherent genre, one whose brevity demands special attention to formal concerns. As Poe maintained, we can sense, can feel narrative structure in the short story with an intensity the novel rarely permits.[2]

The dependence on the power of the ending at the expense of the rest of the story, typical of the second half of the nineteenth century, was an inevitable growth of the inner logic of the short story which Poe had detected. He had in a sense falsified this logic by making it overt and exclusive rather than a frame upon which a variety of effects could be fashioned, and others intensified this error during the supremacy of surprise endings, leading in turn to a reaction: twentieth-century writers strove to suggest incompleteness and continuity and correspondingly altered narrative sequence. Readers had to supply much of what writers had once done for them and had to accept larger degrees of uncertainty and suspension. We might see in "Flowering Judas" that Laura trembles with her frigid "no" while the process that implies change and psychic liberation is at least laid bare for the reader, might see in "Ace in the Hole" not only that Ace is fixed into a druglike dependence on memory but that conditions for his improvement exist, might see in "The Magic Barrel" that the magic of a new earthly life is mysteriously close to a reenactment of the Fall of man. Twentieth-century writers often truncate structure in order to establish theme rather than assuming, as Hawthorne and Melville most commonly did in their short fiction, that closural signals needed to be in place before the reader could deal with thematic suspensions. (Strangely enough, Melville in *Billy Budd* and *The Confidence Man* and Henry James in various novels used longer forms as vehicles for experiments with the truth's ragged edge. By the twentieth century the process is sometimes reversed: Hemingway's early short stories are more structurally innovative than are his novels.) Antistories and traditional narratives such as Cheever's "Artemis, the Honest Well Digger," influenced by contemporary tendencies, push suspension to an extreme. Closure becomes a tonal quality detached from thematic concerns.

Each of these developments demands more of the reader. Short stories have in a sense become shorter, or at least denser, and seem complete in their often fractured forms, because writers have entrusted more to the reader. There is a large body of contemporary critical theory describing this response of the reader, and I share some of the assumptions that theorists such as Wolfgang Iser and Stanley Fish have developed much more formally. My own tendency, to use the set of terms established by Stephen Mailloux in *Interpretive Conventions: The Reader in the Study of American Fiction*, is to focus on sociological rather than psychological models, that is, on models that stress shared experience between readers rather than the reader's individual integration of the text within his psychic needs.[3] The expectation of closure is a communal literary tradition, one that has developed over time and one which the writer assumes his readers share.

I have chosen not to use either the terminology or the theoretical framework that characterizes any of the various reader-response theories or structuralism. The terms I have used—the problem level, natural termination, the antithetical level, the moral or thematic level, encapsulation—I have intentionally kept simple. I have tried to minimize terminology in order more transparently to make the reader sense a part of the reading process of which we are normally unconscious.

Conscious awareness of formal structure and the process has its limits; it may help us understand and appreciate a story, but it is not very helpful if we simply cease to experience because we think we understand. I hope that my readers will seek to use these tools to continue to look for what the writer has done, to find what is unique rather than what is uniformly true of every story. Closure is a highly abstract quality and may be manipulated with infinite variety.

The most forceful example I know to demonstrate a writer's unique approach to closure is Gabriel García Márquez's "The Handsomest Drowned Man in the World" (1968). I think it is appropriate at this point to depart from the North American canon, for now I am arguing for the general use of the concept of closure and not for the function of closure in the development of the American short story. Perhaps I can also justify this deviation by circular design, echoing my original tangent on Boccaccio and Chaucer in the opening, and thus announce my own close.

The simple form and magical effects of García Márquez's story seem to place it at the beginning of the short story's history, in its roots in the tale. It uses familiar closural devices, particularly at the antithetical level, and does not toy in a modern way with the ideas of openness, ambiguity, or extension of the frame. Antithesis dominates: at the beginning of the story all the villagers see no particular significance in the huge drowned man that the children find while playing on the beach and are eager to send him back to sea with minimal ceremony, but by the end, contemplation of the man whose name they decide is Esteban has enlarged the lives first of the women and then the men, endowing them with a sense of beauty. They finally send him back to the sea with reverence, anchorless, "so that he would come back if he wished and whenever he wished."[4] This 180-degree turn in attitude might end the story by itself.

But closure is not an absolute quantity, and no fixed amount of it ends a story. The uniqueness of García Márquez is particularly revealed in the final sentence he appends (two hundred words in the English translation), a sentence that concludes partly by an affirmative natural termination and encapsulation. The sentence strikingly merges the real and the imaginary—"their houses would have wider doors, higher ceilings, and stronger floors so that Esteban's memory could go everywhere without bumping into beams" (p. 104); it echoes previous insults toward the dead man, this time negated and transcended; it suggests the town's new vitality, the painting, the labor; and toward the end of this gargantuan sentence the narrator imagines a captain looking from a ship at the village, pointing to plenitude, to the profusion of flowers, to a captain who

> would have to come down from the bridge in his dress uniform, with his astrolabe, his pole star, and row of war medals and, pointing to the promontory of roses on the horizon, he would say in fourteen languages, look there, where the wind is so peaceful now that it's gone to sleep beneath the beds, over there, where the sun's so bright that the sunflowers don't know which way to turn, yes, over there, that's Esteban's village.[5]

This is a dazzling, breathless close, ending in happy exhaustion. The story has in part been about a lyrical rather than a logical transformation of the attitude of a village, and the final passage expresses by conversational enthusiasm, with interruptions and exaggerations, that very lyricism. The sense of pointing and locating ("look there," "over there") lends this imaginary village a heightened spatial reality while encapsulating it in the distance. The exactness and arbitrary elaborateness of the passage is part of its mystery—war medals and fourteen languages, not the customary three or four or traditional magical number of seven—none of it logically necessary but somehow emotionally essential.

Perhaps in most of this study through my use of five basic structural categories I have given the impression that endings are very cut-and-dried affairs, but they certainly are not. Each ending, at least in the hands of an imaginative writer, is unique, a magical effort that simultaneously rounds off an imaginative world and returns us to our own with reverberations of the world we have momentarily inhabited. A reader sensitive to closure can identify the special strategies writers use to end their works, putting their own stamp on a universal design. Conscious awareness of closure, I hope, puts us nearer, not farther from, this magic.

Notes

Page numbers for primary works have been incorporated into the text whenever possible; the source used is identified in the first reference. Primary works may also be located by using section 3 of the bibliography.

Introduction

1. J. Berg Esenwein, *Writing the Short Story* (New York: Noble and Noble, 1928), p. 211; Marianna Torgovnick, *Closure in the Novel* (Princeton: Princeton University Press, 1981), p. 123.

2. Boris M. Ejxenbaum [Eichenbaum], "O. Henry and the Theory of the Short Story," in Ladislav Matejka and Krystyna Pomorska, eds., *Readings in Russian Poetics: Formalist and Structuralist Views* (Cambridge, Mass.: MIT Press, 1971), p. 231.

3. Edgar Allan Poe, *The Selected Writings of Edgar Allan Poe*, ed. Edward Davidson (Boston: Houghton Mifflin, 1956), p. 449. The version Davidson uses is based on the 1847 revision from *Godey's Lady's Book*. Robert D. Jacobs, in *Poe: Journalist and Critic* (Baton Rouge: Louisiana State University Press, 1969), discusses the sources of Poe's theories of single effect in chapter 13.

4. Poe, *Selected Writings*, p. 453.

5. Brander Matthews was one of the first to adopt Poe's critical theories. See especially *The Philosophy of the Short-story* (New York:

Longmans, Green, 1901); a shorter version appeared in the *London Saturday Review* in 1884 and in *Lippincott's Magazine* in 1885. Two typical early manuals on short-story writing that rely heavily on Poe are Carl Grabo, *The Art of the Short Story* (New York: Charles Scribner's Sons, 1913), and Esenwein, *Writing the Short Story*. Ian Reid, in the last chapter of *The Short Story* (London: Methuen, 1977), is one of the few modern critics to argue that Poe's theories do not describe the genre comprehensively, an issue I discuss more thoroughly in the last chapter.

6. Bernard Malamud, "The Art of Fiction no. LII," *Paris Review* 61 (1975): 57.

7. Austin McGiffert Wright, *The American Short Story in the Twenties* (Chicago: University of Chicago Press, 1961), p. 272.

8. The fullest discussion of Anderson's possible use of Chekhov can be found in Irving Howe, *Sherwood Anderson* (New York: William Sloane, 1951), p. 93. Howe notes Anderson's denials, considers his unreliability in such matters, but does not conclude that Anderson was influenced by Chekhov. Even Cleveland Chase, who maintained that "it seems quite sure that, directly or indirectly, he was influenced" by Chekhov, notes that all of Anderson's influences have been assimilated to the point that source studies throw no light on Anderson's achievement ("In Retrospect," 1927; rpt. in David D. Anderson, *Critical Essays on Sherwood Anderson* [Boston: G. K. Hall, 1981], p. 90).

9. See Frank O'Connor, *The Lonely Voice* (Cleveland: World, 1962), for the discussion of Joyce's influence; Harold M. Hurwitz, "Hemingway's Tutor, Ezra Pound," in Linda Welshimer Wagner, ed., *Ernest Hemingway: Five Decades of Criticism* (East Lansing: Michigan State University Press, 1974); Charles A. Fenton, *The Apprenticeship of Ernest Hemingway: The Early Years* (New York: Viking Press, 1958); and Philip Young, *Ernest Hemingway: A Reconsideration* (University Park, Pa.: Pennsylvania State University Press, 1966), chap. 5. The best brief discussion of Stein's influence specifically, and all the influences in general, can be found in Jackson Benson's concluding essay in Benson, ed., *The Short Stories of Ernest Hemingway: Critical Essays* (Durham, N.C.: Duke University Press, 1975). Michael Reynolds, *Hemingway's Reading, 1910–1940* (Princeton: Princeton University Press, 1981), and Nicholas Joost, *Ernest Hem-*

ingway and the Little Magazines: The Paris Years (Barre, Mass.: Barre Publishers, 1968), offer more detailed accounts.

10. H. C. Bunner, *Made in France: French Tales Retold with a U.S. Twist* (1893; rpt. Freeport, N.Y.: Books for Libraries Press, 1969). James D. Hart, in *The Oxford Companion to American Literature* (New York: Oxford University Press, 1965), p. 118, maintains that in technique Bunner "was so like Maupassant that, when he adapted some of this French master's work . . . he was able to insert an original story without detection," but I can only conclude that no one had Maupassant very fresh in mind.

Chapter 1: Antecedents

1. "The Art of Fiction," in Leon Edel, ed., *Henry James: Selected Fiction* (New York: E. P. Dutton, 1964), p. 590. The essay was originally published in 1888.

2. Robert Louis Stevenson, *The Letters of Robert Louis Stevenson*, ed. Sidney Colvin, 4 vols. (New York: Scribner's, 1911), 3:335–36. The letter, dated September 5, 1891, is addressed to Sidney Colvin. Stevenson is referring to the difficulties of rewriting the story called "High Woods" in the letter; it eventually became "The Beach at Falesa."

3. Barbara Herrnstein Smith, *Poetic Closure: A Study of How Poems End* (Chicago: University of Chicago Press, 1968), p. 2. Several critics (listed in the section on endings in my bibliography) have applied her ideas to other genres. In *Coming to Terms with the Short Story* (Baton Rouge: Louisiana State University Press, 1983), which appeared while I was revising this study for publication, Susan Lohafer argues as I do that closure is essential to the short story, and she applies it even at the level of the sentence.

4. Roland Barthes, *S/Z*, trans. Richard Miller (New York: Hill and Wang, 1974), p. 26.

5. Leonard Meyer, *Emotion and Meaning in Music* (Chicago: University of Chicago Press, 1956), p. 134.

6. Denison Hull, in *Aesop's Fables: Told by Valerius Babrius* (Chicago: University of Chicago Press, 1960), notes that the Babrius text, ca. A.D. 230, did not append morals, but Hull out of deference to tradition includes them.

7. Bernard Malamud, *Idiots First* (New York: Farrar, Straus, 1963), p. 113.

8. T. Coraghessan Boyle, *The Descent of Man* (Boston: Little, Brown, 1979), pp. 83–84.

9. Alan Friedman, *The Turn of the Novel* (New York: Oxford University Press, 1966), pp. 112–13 (Forster),101–2 (Conrad).

10. Edgar Allan Poe, *The Collected Works of Edgar Allan Poe*, ed. Thomas Ollive Mabbott (Cambridge, Mass.: Belknap Press, 1978), 2:29.

11. Boccaccio, *The Decameron*, trans. G. H. McWilliam (Baltimore: Penguin, 1972), p. 268.

12. Geoffrey Chaucer, *The Works of Geoffrey Chaucer*, ed. F. N. Robinson (Boston: Houghton Mifflin, 1961), p. 205.

13. Charles Muscatine, *Chaucer and the French Tradition: A Study in Style and Meaning* (Berkeley and Los Angeles: University of California Press, 1960), p. 242. Robert Adams, in *Strains of Discord: Studies in Literary Openness* (Ithaca: Cornell University Press, 1958), makes a similar point about another classic: "The structure of *Don Quixote* is an extended guerilla action against the recognition of unlimited truth" (p. 84).

14. Henry Seidel Canby, *The Short Story in English* (New York: Henry Holt, 1909), p. 139.

Chapter 2: The Early Nineteenth Century

1. Poe refers to Webber's "Jack Long; or, Shot in the Eye," as "one of the happiest and best-sustained tales I have seen" (Poe, *Selected Writings*, p. 449); the virtue of the story is its proper proportioning within the tradition of the tale. Since an analysis would add nothing new to the present discussion, I have declined further mention of it. Simms's "Murder Will Out" suffers primarily from a misuse of scene and summary. The most striking incident, the one on which Simms lavishes most of his effort, is the appearance of the ghost. What might serve as the formal climax, finding the body of the dead man where the ghost had predicted, is not given any special emphasis, nor is the apprehension of the thief emphasized, through scenic rather than summary treatment, as the climax. Consequently the story does, as Poe claims, dissipate its energy by the end.

2. Hans-Joachim Lang, ed., "The Critical Essays and Stories by John Neal," *Jahrbuch fuer Amerikastudien* (Heidelberg) 7 (1962): 251.

3. Ibid., p. 277. The letter was published in the *Yankee and Boston Literary Gazette*, December 17, 1828. Given Neal's remark, it is no wonder he is now unread; as H. C. Martin has commented in "The Colloquial Tradition in the Novel: John Neal," *New England Quarterly* 32 (1959): 456, "If history has obscured his works, it can only be said that, as usual, it has acted with justice."

4. T. O. Beachcroft, *The Modest Art: A Survey of the Short Story in English* (London: Oxford University Press, 1968), p. 13.

5. Washington Irving, *The Complete Works of Washington Irving* (New York: Thomas Y. Crowell, n.d.), p. 55. I have chosen as the end the Young Italian's final words, without reference to the paragraphs appended by another narrator, the "nervous gentleman," whose comments link this story to those preceding it.

6. Nathaniel Parker Willis, *Dashes at Life with a Free Pencil* (1845; rpt. New York; Garrett Press, 1969), preface to Part I, n.p.

7. Ibid., preface to Part II, n.p. The best analysis of James's views can be found in Torgovnick's *Closure in the Novel*, pp. 4–5.

8. Poe, *Collected Works* 2:397.

9. Canby, *Short Story*, p. 236.

10. Walter Evans, in "'The Fall of the House of Usher' and Poe's Theory of the Tale," *Studies in Short Fiction* 14 (Spring 1977):142, argues that Poe violates his own theories by subordinating plot to "thematic organization of images," thus anticipating twentieth-century short-story practice. I believe Evans's argument about the primacy of images is correct, but I also feel that, at least in the Hawthorne essay, Poe does not raise the issue of the function of plot in relation to other elements.

11. There are, of course, other explanations than the terminal mood for the plotlessness and vagueness. J. O. Bailey, in "What Happens in 'The Fall of the House of Usher,'" *American Literature* 35 (1964):445–66, locates the source of the vagueness in Poe's purposely suppressed account of vampirism. Richard Wilbur, in "The House of Poe," Robert Regan, ed., *Poe: A Collection of Critical Essays* (Englewood Cliffs, N.J.: Prentice-Hall, 1967), p. 103, accounts for the dreamy disconnection as "the effort of the poetic soul to escape all consciousness of the world in dream." An understanding of Poe's

formal concerns complements rather than contradicts the theories of Bailey and Wilbur.

12. Agnes McNeill Donohue, "From Whose Bourn No Traveller Returns: A Reading of 'Roger Malvin's Burial,'" *Nineteenth-Century Fiction* 18 (June 1963):6.

13. Nathaniel Hawthorne, *The Centenary Edition of the Works of Nathaniel Hawthorne* (Columbus: Ohio State University Press, 1974), 10:206. Nina Baym, whose *The Shape of Hawthorne's Career* (Ithaca: Cornell University Press, 1976) is an illuminating account of Hawthorne's short fiction, notes that the accumulating tension of this story differentiates it from the sketches that dominate this period of Hawthorne's writing.

14. Richard P. Adams, "Hawthorne's *Provincial Tales*," *New England Quarterly* 30 (March–December 1957):49.

15. Dieter Schulz, in "Imagination and Self-Imprisonment: The Ending of 'Roger Malvin's Burial,'" *Studies in Short Fiction* 10 (Spring 1973):185, has argued that Reuben's prayer signals his "total withdrawal into the realm of his own subjective consciousness"; Sheldon W. Liebman, in "'Roger Malvin's Burial': Hawthorne's Allegory of the Heart," *Studies in Short Fiction* 12 (Summer 1975):260, argues that Reuben is "a victim of his own morbid imagination"; see also Frederick C. Crews, *The Sins of the Fathers: Hawthorne's Psychological Themes* (New York: Oxford University Press, 1966), pp. 82, 84.

16. Washington Irving, *The Sketch Book*, ed. Haskell Springer (Boston: Twayne, 1978), p. 29.

17. From the December 11, 1824, letter to Henry Brevoort, in Pierre Irving, *The Life and Letters of Washington Irving*, 3 vols. (New York: G. P. Putnam's Sons, 1869), 2:64.

18. Robert Marler, in "From Tale to Short Story: The Emergence of a New Genre in the 1850's," *American Literature* 46 (1974):153–69, notes that Melville wavered throughout his career between older traditions of the tale and the new tradition of the short story. A. W. Plumstead, "Bartleby: Melville's Venture into a New Genre," in Howard P. Vincent, ed., *Bartleby the Scrivener: The Melville Annual* (Kent, Ohio: Kent State University Press, 1966), pp. 82–93, provides a thorough account of how Melville set about teaching himself to write a short story.

19. Herman Melville, *Herman Melville: Selected Tales and Poems*, ed. Richard Chase (New York: Holt, Rinehart and Winston, 1950), p. 99.

Chapter 3: The Later Nineteenth Century

1. *Appleton's Journal* 1 (May 29, 1869):282; Wedmore, "The Short Story," *Nineteenth Century* (March 1898):406–16; both cited in Frank Luther Mott, *A History of American Magazines*, 4th ed., 5 vols. (Cambridge, Mass.: Harvard University Press, 1970), 3:226. A good assessment of short-story theory during this period is provided by Walter Evans, "Nineteenth-century American Theory of the Short Story: The Dual Tradition," *Orbis Litterarum* 34 (1979): 314–30.

2. Claude M. Simpson, ed., *The Local Colorists: American Short Stories, 1857–1900* (New York: Harper & Brothers, 1960), p. 169.

3. Graves Glenwood Clark, "The Development of the Surprise Ending in the American Short Story from Washington Irving through O. Henry" (Ph.D. dissertation, Columbia University, 1930).

4. Mott, *History of American Magazines*, 3:228.

5. Clark, "Development of the Surprise Ending," p. 152.

6. Willis, *Dashes at Life*, p. 153.

7. Thomas Bailey Aldrich, *Marjorie Daw and Other People* (Boston: Houghton Mifflin, 1915), p. 17.

8. Justifications for surprise endings have been offered. Elliott L. Smith and Andrew W. Hart, in *The Short Story: A Contemporary Looking Glass* (New York: Random House, 1981), suggest in reference to "Marjorie Daw" that "perhaps there is an even darker side" of the young attorney. "Maybe for some unknown and perhaps subconscious reason, he even comes to the point of trying to punish his old friend" (p. 238), but Aldrich establishes nothing of the background of their friendship; Smith and Hart's comments apply methods derived from reading psychological fiction, the dominant form of the twentieth century. For a justification of Bierce, see Gerald Barrett and Thomas Erskine, eds., *From Fiction to Film: Ambrose Bierce's "An Occurrence at Owl Creek Bridge"* (Encino, Calif.: Dickenson Publishing, 1973), especially Erskine's article, pp. 69–75.

9. Edward J. O'Brien, *The Advance of the American Short Story* (New York: Dodd, Mead, 1931), p. 143.

10. O. Henry, "A Lickpenny Lover," *The Voice of the City* (1908; rpt. Garden City, N.Y.: Doubleday, 1920), p. 29.

11. Terry Heller, in "The Telltale Hair: A Critical Study of William Faulkner's 'A Rose for Emily,' " *Arizona Quarterly* 28 (Winter 1972):301–18, provides a good summary of previous criticism and a new focus for the story. Particularly interesting in this context is Heller's observation that at the end the reader confronts more, not less, of a mystery about Emily, a point that I feel reverses what customarily happens in the surprise tradition.

12. Edith Wharton, *The Collected Short Stories of Edith Wharton*, ed. R. W. B. Lewis (New York: Charles Scribner's Sons, 1968), 2:833.

13. Mark Twain, *Great Short Works of Mark Twain*, ed. Justin Kaplan (New York: Harper & Row, 1967), p. 182.

14. Ibid., p. 80. I have selected Kaplan's edition, which like most other reprints is based on Albert Bigelow Paine's. Another version, "Jim Smiley and His Jumping Frog," is printed in the Center for Editions of American Authors–sanctioned *Early Tales and Sketches*, vol. 2, ed. Edgar Marquess Branch et al. (Berkeley and Los Angeles: University of California Press, 1981); this Iowa-California edition, based on the 1865 *New York Saturday Press* text, shows the marks of the story's original connection to a request for a story from Artemus Ward. I do not believe it is as polished as later versions which Twain himself supervised. Pages 262–72 in the Iowa-California edition thoroughly discuss the history of the text.

15. Sarah Orne Jewett, *The Country of the Pointed Firs and Other Stories* (Garden City, N.Y.: Doubleday, 1956), p. 161.

16. Eric Solomon, in *Stephen Crane: From Parody to Realism* (Cambridge, Mass.: Harvard University Press, 1966), establishes Crane's habit of parody but without reference to the short story as a genre.

17. Stephen Crane, *The University of Virginia Edition of The Works of Stephen Crane*, ed. Fredson Bowers, vol. 5, *Tales of Adventure* (Charlottesville: University Press of Virginia, 1970), p. 109.

18. See Clark Griffith's account of the endings of "The Open Boat" and *The Red Badge of Courage* in "Stephen Crane and the Ironic Last Word," *Philological Quarterly* 47 (January 1968):83–91.

Chapter 4: Converging Closure and the Theory of Openness

1. On the subject of his debt to Maupassant, James noted: "It seemed harmless sport simply to turn that situation round—to shift, in other words, the ground of the horrid mistake, making this a matter not of a false treasure supposed to be true and precious, but of a real treasure supposed to be false and hollow" (Henry James, *The Novels and Tales of Henry James*, 24 vols. [New York: Charles Scribner's Sons, 1908], 16:x; hereafter cited as the New York Edition). Two critics, Francis Steegmuller in *Maupassant: A Lion in the Path* (New York: Random House, 1949), and T. M. Segnitz in more detail in "The Actual Genesis of Henry James's 'Paste,'" *American Literature* 36 (May 1964): 216–19, have noted that James, instead of borrowing the plot of "La Parure," used the plot of another Maupassant story, "Les Bijoux." On the topic of the quality of the ending, Ian Reid, unlike most critics, argues in *The Short Story*, pp. 60–61, that the surprise establishes rather than undercuts the value of the story.

2. "The Art of Fiction," in Edel, ed., *Henry James, Selected Fiction*, p. 596.

3. Ibid., p. 590.

4. Henry James, *The Notebooks of Henry James*, ed. F. O. Matthiessen and Kenneth B. Murdock (1947; rpt. New York: Oxford University Press, 1961), p. 64. In the final version the main character became a male.

5. Ibid., pp. 102–4.

6. Torgovnick, *Closure in the Novel*, p. 123.

7. Torgovnick uses the 1881 edition. As she points out, the revised ending of the New York Edition, which adds another paragraph, is "less ambiguous" and "less demanding" (p. 136).

8. William Peden, *The American Short Story* (Norman: University of Oklahoma Press, 1973), p. 156. Sean O'Faolain in *The Short Story* (1951; rpt. New York: Devin-Adair, 1964), pp. 210–12, is corrosive on James's skill as a short-story writer, particularly because of the excess verbiage in a story such as "The Beast in the Jungle." Beachcroft in *Modest Art* argues that James was "the very reverse of a short-story writer; he is a producer of elaborate discussions about stories" (p. 153).

9. James, *Notebooks*, p. 212. The emphasis is James's.

10. The argument that James did not conceive of short stories as a unique genre is most thoroughly presented in Hildegard Domaniecki, *Zum Problem literarischer Oekonomie: Henry James' Erzaehlungen zwischen Markt und Kunst* (Stuttgart: J. B. Metzlersche, 1974), p. 119. In a footnote (n. 69, p. 269) Domaniecki argues that Matthews's essay *(Philosophy of the Short-story)* was written in part to reject James's theories in "The Art of Fiction." Domaniecki's book provides a more thorough account of the theoretical background behind James's short fiction than can be found in the prefaces to Leon Edel's twelve-volume edition of James's tales, in James Kraft, *The Early Tales of Henry James* (Carbondale: Southern Illinois University Press, 1969), or in Krishna Baldev Vaid, *Technique in the Tales of Henry James* (Cambridge, Mass.: Harvard University Press, 1964).

11. Henry James, *The Complete Tales of Henry James*, ed. Leon Edel (Philadelphia: J. B. Lippincott, 1961) 2:8. Except for "The Bundle of Letters," for which I selected the New York Edition, all subsequent citations to James's short stories are to the Edel edition. Edel's edition selects the first book publication as the standard text; the New York Edition has James's late revisions.

12. *Hubert Crackanthorpe: Last Studies* (London: William Heinemann, 1897) pp. xviii–xix.

13. Henry James, "The Story-Teller at Large: Mr. Henry Harland," *Fortnightly Review* 69 (April 1898), rpt. in *The American Essays*, ed. Leon Edel (New York: Vintage, 1956), p. 190. A portion is also reprinted in James E. Miller, ed., *Theory of Fiction* (Lincoln: University of Nebraska Press, 1972), pp. 99–101.

14. James, *Notebooks*, p. 118.

15. Henry James, *The Art of the Novel*, ed. R. P. Blackmur (1907; rpt. New York: Scribner's, 1962), p. 6.

16. James, *The Novels and Tales of Henry James* (New York Edition), 14:483.

17. Miller, ed., *Theory of Fiction*, p. 102. The original passage, which refers to "The Middle Years," comes from the 1909 Preface to *The Author of Beltraffio*.

18. James, *Art of the Novel*, pp. 127–28. The passage quoted refers to a novel, *The Spoils of Poynton*.

19. H. G. Ruthrof, "A Note on Henry James's Psychological Real-

ism and the Concept of Brevity," *Studies in Short Fiction* 12 (Fall 1975):373.

20. Roy Basler in *Sex, Symbolism, and Psychology in Literature* (New York: Octagon Books, 1967), pp. 143–59, offers a different interpretation: the narrator wills Ligeia back to life and from the beginning has been designing a tomb, not a bridal chamber, for Rowena.

21. Wright, *American Short Story,* p. 273.

22. Ibid., pp. 266–67.

23. Sherwood Anderson, *Winesburg, Ohio,* ed. Malcolm Cowley (New York: Viking Press, 1960), p. 234.

24. See especially Robert Caserio's *Plot, Story and the Novel: From Dickens and Poe to the Modern Period* (Princeton: Princeton University Press, 1979).

25. Arthur F. Kinney, *Faulkner's Narrative Poetics: Style as Vision* (Amherst: University of Massachusetts Press, 1978), p. xiii. Because I emphasize familiar narrative elements in stories of all types, I do not distinguish between what Eileen Baldeshwiler calls lyrical and epical stories. (See "The Lyrical Short Story: The Sketch of a History," in Charles E. May, ed., *Short Story Theories* [Athens: Ohio University Press, 1976], pp. 202–13). Even lyrical stories, I would argue, display the rhythms of beginnings, middles, and ends.

Chapter 5: The Twentieth Century: New Forms

1. Sherwood Anderson, *A Story Teller's Story,* ed. Ray Lewis White (Cleveland: Press of Case Western Reserve University, 1968), pp. 280, 255.

2. Anderson, *Winesburg, Ohio,* p. 33. William Phillips, "How Sherwood Anderson Wrote *Winesburg, Ohio,*" in Ray Lewis White, ed., *The Achievement of Sherwood Anderson: Essays in Criticism* (Chapel Hill: University of North Carolina Press, 1966), offers details about the composition and dating of the story.

3. Sherwood Anderson, *Death in the Woods and Other Stories* (New York: Liveright, 1933), p. 22.

4. Eugene Current-Garcia and Walton R. Patrick, *American Short Stories,* 4th ed. (Glenview, Ill.: Scott, Foresman, 1981), p. 323.

5. Anderson, *A Story Teller's Story,* p. 277.

6. Ray Lewis White, ed., *Sherwood Anderson/Gertrude Stein: Correspondence and Personal Essays* (Chapel Hill: University of North Carolina Press, 1972), pp. 26–27.

7. Katherine Anne Porter, interview with Barbara Thompson in *Writers at Work: The Paris Review Interviews*, 2d ser. (New York: Viking Press, 1963), p. 151.

8. Ibid., p. 152.

9. Beverly Gross, "The Poetic Narrative: A Reading of 'Flowering Judas,'" *Style* 2 (Spring 1968):138; David Madden, "The Charged Image in Katherine Anne Porter's 'Flowering Judas,'" *Studies in Short Fiction* 7 (Spring 1970):283.

10. Katherine Anne Porter, *The Collected Stories of Katherine Anne Porter* (New York: Harcourt, Brace, and World, 1965), p. 91.

11. Leon Gottfried, "Death's Other Kingdom: Dantesque and Theological Symbolism in 'Flowering Judas,'" *PMLA* 84 (January 1969):112–24.

12. Ernest Hemingway, *The Short Stories of Ernest Hemingway* (New York: Charles Scribner's Sons, 1966), p. 179.

13. Ernest Hemingway, *Death in the Afternoon* (New York: Charles Scribner's Sons, 1932), p. 192. Years later Hemingway maintained the same arguments about the iceberg and the effect of omissions in the interview by George Plimpton, *Writers at Work*, p. 235.

14. Ernest Hemingway, *A Moveable Feast* (New York: Scribner's, 1964), p. 75.

15. Carlos Baker in *Ernest Hemingway: A Life Story* (New York: Charles Scribner's Sons, 1969), p. 109, provides the biographical information that lies behind the story.

16. Hemingway, *Death in the Afternoon*, p. 182. One story to which Hemingway added the "wow" was "A Canary for One," in which the narrator tells of an American lady with whom he and his wife shared a train ride, a lady bringing a canary for her daughter, whose marriage to a Swiss she had prevented because of her high opinion of the fidelity of American suitors. The narrator, himself an American, admits to the reader in the final line that he and his wife were planning to set up separate residences after getting off the train.

17. Ernest Hemingway, *The Green Hills of Africa* (New York: Charles Scribner's Sons, 1935), p. 20. In the 1963 Plimpton interview he admitted that he was "sounding off about American literature

with a humorless Austrian character who was forcing me to talk
when I wanted to do something else" (*Writers at Work*, p. 234), but the
judgment seems nonetheless permanent.

18. The pattern of these endings is partly determined by the function of these stories within *In Our Time*. Many of the stories, though,
were published individually with the same endings, indicating that
they were perceived by editors at least as reasonably complete units.
In ending "The Doctor and the Doctor's Wife" with Nick, Hemingway may be emphasizing connections with the previous story, "Indian Camp," and the one following, "The End of Something." The
major study of interrelated stories is Forrest L. Ingram's *Representative Short Story Cycles of the Twentieth Century: Studies in a Literary
Genre* (The Hague: Mouton, 1971).

19. John Hagopian, "Cat in the Rain," *College English*, vol. 24;
rpt. in Ernest Hemingway, *The Short Stories of Ernest Hemingway:
Critical Essays*, ed. Jackson Benson (Durham, N.C.: Duke University Press, 1975), p. 232. Carlos Baker, in *Hemingway: The Writer as
Artist* (Princeton: Princeton University Press, 1963), p. 136, argues
that the cat "is finally sent up to her by the kindly old inn-keeper
whose sympathetic deference is greater than that of the young husband," differing with Hagopian about the cat but pointing to the
contrast between the husband and the padrone.

20. Baker, *Hemingway: The Writer as Artist*, p. 189; Arthur Waldhorn *A Reader's Guide to Ernest Hemingway* (New York: Farrar, Straus
and Giroux, 1972), p. 50.

21. Virgil Hutton, "The Short Happy Life of Macomber," in
Hemingway, *Short Stories,* ed. Benson, p. 244; Warren Beck, "The
Shorter Happy Life of Mrs. Macomber," *Modern Fiction Studies* 1
(November 1955):28–37.

22. Robert B. Holland, "Macomber and the Critics," *Studies in
Short Fiction* 5 (Winter 1968):171–78. Holland makes the point em-
phatically and chastens critics who have ignored the plain evidence of
the text.

23. Beck, "Shorter Happy Life of Mrs. Macomber," p. 36; Anne
Greco, "Margot Macomber: 'Bitch Goddess,' Exonerated,"
Fitzgerald/Hemingway Annual (1972):273–80.

24. John Hill, "Robert Wilson: Hemingway's Judge in 'Macomber,'" *University Review* 35 (1968):132.

25. R. S. Crane, *The Idea of the Humanities*, 2 vols. (Chicago: University of Chicago Press, 1967), 2:316.

Chapter 6: The Twentieth Century: Extending the Frame

1. Truman Capote, *Selected Writings* (New York: Random House, 1963), p. 33.

2. Joyce Carol Oates, *The Wheel of Love and Other Stories* (New York: Vanguard Press, 1965), p. 37.

3. Quoted in Ruth M. Vande Kieft, "Judgment in the Fiction of Flannery O'Connor," *Sewanee Review* 76 (Spring 1968):345.

4. Ibid., p. 344.

5. Flannery O'Connor, *The Complete Stories* (New York: Farrar, Straus and Giroux, 1971), p. 525.

6. "The Art of Fiction, XLIII: John Updike," *Paris Review* 12, no. 45 (1968):96.

7. John Updike, *The Same Door* (New York: Alfred A. Knopf, 1972), p. 14.

8. Bernard Malamud, *The Magic Barrel* (New York: Farrar, Straus and Giroux, 1966), pp. 213–14.

9. Lionel Trilling, *The Experience of Literature* (Garden City, N.Y.: Doubleday, 1967), p. 809.

10. See in particular Marcus Klein in *After Alienation* (Freeport, N.Y.: Books for Libraries Press, 1970): Salzman, he argues, "will eventually trick Leo into knowing that love and life and suffering and lowliness [sic?] and death inhabit the same place. When Leo accepts that much, violins and candles will revolve in the sky, he will in effect be ordained, and he will in effect become a Jew" (pp. 277–78); see also Michael Story, who considers Stella "the perfect complement of Leo's ascetic nature" ("Pinye Salzman, Pan and 'The Magic Barrel,'" *Studies in Short Fiction* 18 [Spring 1982]:183).

11. The similarity of "That Evening Sun" to "The Killers" seems to have been noticed first by Ray B. West, Jr., in *The Short Story in America* (Chicago: Henry Regnery, 1952), p. 98. See Norman Holmes Pearson, "Faulkner's Three 'Evening Suns,'" *Yale University Library Gazette* 29 (October 1954):61–70, for a fuller explanation, as well as a history of the three versions of the text. Leo M. J. Mang-

laviti, in "Faulkner's 'That Evening Sun' and Mencken's 'Best Editorial Judgment,'" *American Literature* 43 (January 1972):649–54, uses Mencken correspondence now available at the New York Public Library to confirm and expand Pearson's estimations about Mencken's editorial influence.

12. John Cheever, *The Stories of John Cheever* (New York: Alfred A. Knopf, 1978), p. 155.

13. Hemingway, *Short Stories*, p. 289.

14. Avrahm Yarmolinsky, ed., *The Portable Chekhov* (New York: Viking Press, 1965), p. 433.

15. William Faulkner, *The Collected Stories of William Faulkner* (New York: Random House, 1950), p. 294.

16. Cleanth Brooks, *A Shaping Joy: Studies in the Writer's Craft* (New York: Harcourt Brace Jovanovich, 1971), p. 237; Olga W. Vickery, *The Novels of William Faulkner: A Critical Interpretation* (Baton Rouge: Louisiana State University Press, 1964), p. 301.

17. Vickery, *Novels of Faulkner*, p. 301; Jim Lee, "The Problem of Nancy in Faulkner's 'That Evening Sun,'" *South Central Bulletin* 21 (Winter, 1961):50.

18. John V. Hagopian and Martin Dolch, *Insight I: Analyses of American Literature* (Frankfurt am Main: Hirschgraben Verlag, 1964), p. 54. Joseph Blotner, in *Faulkner: A Biography* (New York: Random House, 1974), p. 565, notes of the manuscript version, and by implication the later versions, that death is "the unspoken but clear implication."

19. Brooks, *A Shaping Joy*, p. 234; May Cameron Brown, "Voice in 'That Evening Sun,'" *Mississippi Quarterly* 29 (1976):355.

20. John Hermann, "Faulkner's Heart's Darling in 'That Evening Sun,'" *Studies in Short Fiction* 7 (Spring 1970):323.

21. Hagopian and Dolch, *Insight I,* p. 54. May Cameron Brown's article provides a thorough discussion of the extent of Quentin's knowledge.

22. Pearson, "Faulkner's Three 'Evening Suns,'" p. 66.

23. Stephen Whicher, "Compson's Nancies, a Note on *The Sound and the Fury* and 'That Evening Sun,'" *American Literature* 26 (May 1954):253–55. Extratextual information does not help to resolve the problem of the ending. John B. Cullen, in *Old Times in the Faulkner Country* (Chapel Hill: University of North Carolina Press, 1961), p.

72, comments that "Faulkner wrote about events that actually happened, but left them only expected and dreaded in the story. Nancy was terribly afraid that her husband Jesus would kill her; the murder did not occur in the story. It did in life." But Cullen notes throughout that Faulkner was under no obligation to be faithful to incidents he had heard or seen. Faulkner has admitted the essential identity of Nancy from this story and Nancy Manigoe from *Requiem for a Nun* (Frederick L. Gwynn and Joseph L. Blotner, eds., *Faulkner in the University* [New York: Vintage, 1959], p. 79), but that too, as several commentators have noted, proves nothing. If we ask Faulkner to be consistent, Quentin could not be narrating this story: he is twenty-four at the time he tells it, but he died at twenty-one in *The Sound and the Fury*.

24. Philip Momberger, "Faulkner's 'The Village' and 'That Evening Sun': The Tale in Context," *Southern Literary Journal* 11 (Fall 1978):30–31.

25. Gwynn and Blotner, eds., *Faulkner in the University*, p. 21.

Chapter 7: Antistory and Story: From Tralfamadore to Tale

1. Kurt Vonnegut, Jr., *Slaughterhouse-Five* (New York: Dell, 1969), p. 76. Joseph Frank's well-known arguments about spatial form, collected in *The Widening Gyre: Crisis and Mastery in Modern Literature* (New Brunswick: Rutgers University Press, 1963), pp. 3–62, are a similar attempt to account for simultaneity. Some critics (see Gross on "Flowering Judas" in Chapter 5) have applied Frank's theories to the short story.

2. Poe, *Selected Writings*, p. 448.

3. Sansford Pinsker (interviewer), "Speaking about Short Fiction: An Interview with Joyce Carol Oates," *Studies in Short Fiction* 18 (Summer 1981):241.

4. Robert Coover, *Pricksongs and Descants* (New York: E. P. Dutton, 1969), p. 237.

5. Ibid., p. 239. The difficulties of the text seem to have plagued not only the reader but the author and proofreaders as well—the 1969 Dutton edition lists Mrs. Tucker as the speaker of the line "Did you hear the news about the babysitter?", an error that has been rectified

in reprints of the story such as the one in R. V. Cassill's *Norton Anthology of Short Fiction*, 2d ed. (New York: W. W. Norton, 1981), p. 344. I have made the correction here.

6. Donald Barthelme, *Unspeakable Practices, Unnatural Acts* (New York: Farrar, Straus and Giroux, 1968), p. 16.

7. William Gass, *In the Heart of the Heart of the Country and Other Stories* (New York: Harper & Row, 1968), p. 173.

8. Annette Grant, "John Cheever: The Art of Fiction," *Paris Review* 17 (Fall 1976):51.

9. John Cheever, *The Stories of John Cheever* (New York: Alfred A. Knopf, 1978), p. 650.

Chapter 8: Conclusion

1. Reid, *The Short Story*, pp. 54–55.

2. I realize that one can exaggerate the argument for both the uniqueness of Poe's discovery of requirements of the genre and for the separateness of the short story from other narrative modes. As a corrective one need only consult William Ryding, *The Structure of Medieval Narrative* (The Hague: Mouton, 1971), which has demonstrated that Poe's application of Aristotelian principles to the short story parallels Tasso's to the epic. The function of logical sequence, Tasso had argued, was to facilitate the power of memory, thus allowing the reader to draw connections between the beginning and ending. As for the argument of separateness, whether we shall call the short story unique, as does Poe, or continuous, as does James, is largely a matter of taste and the dictates of one's argument. I prefer to think that the short story embodies the same laws as longer narrative modes, but more obviously, and in that sense is unique.

3. Stephen Mailloux, *Interpretive Conventions: The Reader in the Study of American Fiction* (Ithaca: Cornell University Press, 1982), p. 41.

4. Gabriel García Márquez, *Leaf Storm and Other Stories*, trans. Gregory Rabassa (New York: Harper & Row, 1972), p. 103.

5. Ibid., p. 104. Rabassa's translation nearly replicates the rhythms of the original Spanish: "el capitán tuviera que bajar de su alcázar con su uniforme de gala, con su astrolabio, su estrella polar y su ristra de medallas de guerra, y señalando el promontorio de rosas

en el horizonte del Caribe dijera en catorce idiomas, miren allá, donde el viento es ahora tan manso que se queda a dormir debajo de las camas, allá, donde el sol brilla tanto que no saben hacia dónde girar los girasoles, sí, allá, es el pueblo de Esteban" *(Todos los cuentos por Gabriel Garcia Marquez* [Barcelona: Plaza & Janes, 1976], p. 245).

Selected Bibliography

The bibliography is divided into three sections: (1) Endings, (2) Short-Story Theory and History, and (3) Primary Texts. I have not attempted to list books on general narrative theory that are not used in the text. Books and magazine articles on specific writers, particularly those that have influenced my arguments, are listed in the notes to the chapters rather than here; readers interested in more complete listings of articles should consult Warren Walker's *Twentieth-Century Short Story Explication: Interpretations, 1900–1975, of Short Fiction since 1800*, 3d ed. (Hamden, Conn.: Shoe String Press, 1977), and the annual updates in *Studies in Short Fiction*.

I have generally cited the most authoritative primary texts available. Reasons for exceptions (Twain, for example) are explained in the notes. For many minor and a few major nineteenth-century writers and many contemporary ones, authoritative texts have not yet been established, so I have tried to cite texts that are widely available.

Endings

Adams, Robert. *Strains of Discord: Studies in Literary Openness*. Ithaca: Cornell University Press, 1958.

Ejxenbaum [Eichenbaum], Boris M. "O. Henry and the Theory of the Short Story." In *Readings in Russian Poetics: Formalist and Struc-*

turalist Views, edited by Ladislav Matejka and Krystyna Pomorska. Cambridge, Mass.: MIT Press, 1971.

Friedman, Alan. *The Turn of the Novel*. New York: Oxford University Press, 1966.

Kermode, Frank. *The Sense of an Ending: Studies in the Theory of Fiction*. London: Oxford University Press, 1966.

Miller, D. A. *Narrative and Its Discontents: Problems of Closure in the Traditional Novel*. Princeton: Princeton University Press, 1981.

Miller, J. Hillis. "The Problematic of Ending in Narrative." *Nineteenth Century Fiction* 33 (June 1978):3–7. This entire issue is devoted to articles on endings.

Richter, David H. *The Fable's End: Completeness and Closure in Rhetorical Fiction*. Chicago: University of Chicago Press, 1974.

Smith, Barbara Herrnstein. *Poetic Closure: A Study of How Poems End*. Chicago: University of Chicago Press, 1968.

Torgovnick, Marianna. *Closure in the Novel*. Princeton: Princeton University Press, 1981.

Short-Story Theory and History

Bates, H. E. *The Modern Short Story: A Critical Survey*. Boston: Writer, 1965.

Beachcroft, T. O. *The Modest Art: A Survey of the Short Story in English*. London: Oxford University Press, 1968.

Canby, Henry Seidel. *The Short Story in English*. New York: Henry Holt, 1909.

Clark, Graves Glenwood. "The Development of the Surprise Ending in the American Short Story from Washington Irving through O. Henry." Ph.D. dissertation, Columbia University, 1930.

Current-Garcia, Eugene, and Walton R. Patrick. *American Short Stories*. 4th ed. Glenview, Ill.: Scott, Foresman, 1981.

Dollerup, Cay. "The Concepts of 'Tension,' 'Intensity,' and 'Suspense' in Short-Story Theory." *Orbis Litterarum* 25 (1970):314–37.

Evans, Walter. "Nineteenth-century American Theory of the Short Story: The Dual Tradition." *Orbis Litterarum* 34 (1979):314–30.

Harris, Wendell V. *British Short Fiction in the Nineteenth Century*. Detroit: Wayne State University Press, 1979.

Lohafer, Susan. *Coming to Terms with the Short Story*. Baton Rouge: Louisiana State University Press, 1983.

Marler, Robert F. "From Tale to Short Story: The Emergence of a New Genre in the 1850's." *American Literature* 46 (1974):153–69.

Matthews, Brander. *The Philosophy of the Short-Story*. New York: Longmans, Green, 1901.

May, Charles E. *Short Story Theories*. Athens: Ohio University Press, 1976.

Mott, Frank Luther. *A History of American Magazines*. 5 vols. 4th ed. Cambridge, Mass.: Harvard University Press, 1970.

O'Brien, Edward J. *The Advance of the American Short Story*. New York: Dodd, Mead, 1931.

O'Connor, Frank. *The Lonely Voice*. Cleveland: World, 1962.

O'Faolain, Sean. *The Short Story*. 1951; rpt. New York: Devin-Adair, 1964.

Pattee, Frederick Lewis. *The Development of the American Short Story: An Historical Survey*. New York: Harper & Brothers, 1923.

Peden, William. *The American Short Story*. Norman: University of Oklahoma Press, 1973.

Reid, Ian. *The Short Story*. London: Methuen, 1977.

Rohrberger, Mary. *Hawthorne and the Modern Short Story: A Study in Genre*. The Hague: Mouton, 1966.

Simpson, Claude M., ed. *The Local Colorists: American Short Stories, 1875–1900*. New York: Harper & Brothers, 1960.

Voss, Arthur. *The American Short Story: A Critical Survey*. Boston: Houghton Mifflin, 1975.

West, Ray B., Jr. *The Short Story in America, 1900–1950*. Chicago: Henry Regnery, 1952.

Wright, Austin McGiffert. *The American Short Story in the Twenties*. Chicago: University of Chicago Press, 1961.

Primary Texts

Aldrich, Thomas Bailey. *Majorie Daw and Other People*. Boston: Houghton Mifflin, 1915.

Anderson, Sherwood. *Winesburg, Ohio*. Edited by Malcolm Cowley. New York: Viking Press, 1960.

Barth, John. *Lost in the Funhouse*. Garden City, N.Y.: Doubleday, 1968.

Barthelme, Donald. *Unspeakable Practices, Unnatural Acts*. New York: Farrar, Straus and Giroux, 1968.

Boccaccio. *The Decameron*. Translated by G. H. McWilliam. Baltimore: Penguin, 1972.

Boyle, T. Coraghessan. *The Descent of Man*. Boston: Little, Brown, 1979.

Bunner, H. C. *Made in France: French Tales Retold with a U.S. Twist*. 1893; rpt. Freeport, N.Y.: Books for Libraries Press, 1969.

Capote, Truman. *Selected Writings*. New York: Random House, 1963.

Chaucer, Geoffrey. *The Works of Geoffrey Chaucer*. Edited by F. N. Robinson. Boston: Houghton Mifflin, 1961.

Cheever, John. *The Stories of John Cheever*. New York: Alfred A. Knopf, 1978.

Coover, Robert. *Pricksongs and Descants*. New York: E. P. Dutton, 1969.

Crane, Stephen. *The University of Virginia Edition of The Works of Stephen Crane*. Edited by Fredson Bowers. Vol.5, *Tales of Adventure*. Charlottesville: University Press of Virginia, 1970.

Faulkner, William. *The Collected Stories of William Faulkner*. New York: Random House, 1950.

García Márquez, Gabriel. *Leaf Storm and Other Stories*. Translated by Gregory Rabassa. New York: Harper & Row, 1972.

Gass, William. *In the Heart of the Heart of the Country and Other Stories*. New York: Harper & Row, 1968.

Hawthorne, Nathaniel. *The Centenary Edition of the Works of Nathaniel Hawthorne*. Vols. 10 and 11. Columbus: Ohio State University Press, 1974.

Hemingway, Ernest. *The Short Stories of Ernest Hemingway*. New York: Charles Scribner's Sons, 1966.

Henry, O. *The Voice of the City*. 1908; rpt. Garden City, N.Y.: Doubleday, 1920.

Irving, Washington. *The Sketch Book*. Edited by Haskell Springer. Boston: Twayne, 1978.

——. *Tales of a Traveler*. In *The Complete Works of Washington Irving*. New York: Thomas Y. Crowell, n.d.

James, Henry. *The Complete Tales of Henry James*. Edited by Leon Edel. Vols. 9 and 11. Philadelphia: J. B. Lippincott, 1961.

———. *The Novels and Tales of Henry James*. Vols. 14 and 16. New York: Charles Scribner's Sons, 1908.

Jewett, Sarah Orne. *The Country of the Pointed Firs and Other Stories*. Garden City, N.Y.: Doubleday, 1956.

Malamud, Bernard. *The Magic Barrel*. New York: Farrar, Straus and Giroux, 1966.

Melville, Herman. *Herman Melville: Selected Tales and Poems*. Edited by Richard Chase. New York: Holt, Rinehart and Winston, 1950.

Oates, Joyce Carol. *The Wheel of Love and Other Stories*. New York: Vanguard Press, 1965.

O'Connor, Flannery. *The Complete Stories*. New York: Farrar, Straus and Giroux, 1971.

[Page, Thomas Nelson]. *The Local Colorists: American Short Stories, 1857–1900*. Edited by Claude M. Simpson. New York: Harper & Brothers, 1960.

Poe, Edgar Allan. *The Collected Works of Edgar Allan Poe*. Edited by Thomas Ollive Mabbott. Vol. 2. Cambridge, Mass.: Belknap Press, 1978.

Porter, Katherine Anne. *The Collected Stories of Katherine Anne Porter*. New York: Harcourt, Brace, and World, 1965.

Twain, Mark. *Great Short Works of Mark Twain*. Edited by Justin Kaplan. New York: Harper & Row, 1967.

Updike, John. *The Same Door*. New York: Alfred A. Knopf, 1972.

Wharton, Edith. *The Collected Short Stories of Edith Wharton*. Edited by R. W. B. Lewis. Vol. 2. New York: Scribner's Sons, 1968.

Willis, Nathaniel Parker. *Dashes at Life with a Free Pencil*. 1845; rpt. New York: Garrett Press, 1969.

Index

189